FOR A WORLD
LIKE OURS

Studies in I Corinthians

FOR A WORLD LIKE OURS

Studies in I Corinthians

by
James L. Boyer

BMH BOOKS

Winona Lake, Indiana

Library of Congress Catalog Card Number: 70-174807

Baker Book House ISBN: 0-8010-0553-1

Copyright, 1971, by
BMH Books

Baker Book House and BMH Books — co-publishers

Second printing, May 1975

To

My Beloved Wife

Velma

who for forty years has been to me

a Faithful Help-meet

(the precise one that I needed)

. . . . .

and to

the Berean Bible Class

of the

Winona Lake Brethren Church

which for almost twenty years has been to me

a Much Appreciated Opportunity

to

Teach the Word of God

. . . . .

is this book lovingly dedicated

FOREWORD

HERMAN A. HOYT

James L. Boyer brings to the Christian reading public a fresh investigation of the First Epistle of Paul to the Corinthians. A reading of this treatise impresses one with the practicality of this epistle in this day, after the passing of nineteen centuries. With amazing skill the author clearly unfolds the message of this book and makes its application to the Christian society of our times.

Dr. Boyer's background in Greek literature and his intense study of the Greek language over a period of some forty years qualify him to do a scholarly piece of work on this epistle. It becomes quite evident that his familiarity with the original language enables him to give those touches to and add such insights, in the exposition of his message, that would ordinarily elude the average student.

Being a student of archaeology, and also having had opportunity to spend prolonged periods of study in Bible lands, he reproduces the setting of this epistle in living and vibrant form. This makes it possible for the reader to feel the intensity of the problems just as they developed among the believers at Corinth. This creative quality helps the reader to project the message into situations that prevail today.

With most illuminating exposition, the writer opens up the message of Chapters 12 to 14 dealing with spiritual gifts. He provides the reader with a masterful interpretative paraphrase of Chapter 13. Then with keen insight he strikes at the heart of the problem that existed in the church at Corinth in the area of speaking in tongues. Saints who are troubled over the so-called modern recrudescence of this spiritual phenomenon will get a great deal of assistance from the explanation of Paul's instruction.

It is both a privilege and a pleasure to write this foreword for Dr. Boyer. I have known him for more than forty years, both as a fellow student and for many years as a colleague. He is eminently qualified both spiritually and scholastically to prepare a volume such as this one. It is my hope that this is merely one of many books that will appear from his pen in the near future. His style, clarity, and perception will minister blessing to thousands who have the good fortune to peruse his writing.

PREFACE

If Paul were to write a letter to the evangelical, Bible-believing churches of late twentieth century America, I believe it would be much like I Corinthians. Their world was like our world: the same thirst for intellectualism, the same permissiveness toward moral standards, the same fascination for the spectacular. And their church was like our churches: proud, affluent, materialistic, fiercely eager for intellectual and social acceptance by the world, doctrinally orthodox but morally and practically conforming to the world.

It is my firm belief that the Bible, the Holy Scripture, is the tool God has put into our hands to do *all* His work, whether that work is the salvation of sinners (II Tim. 3:15), or the profit of the saints (II Tim. 3:16), or the equipping of the worker (II Tim. 3:17). First Corinthians is a tool primarily for the profit of the saints — by doctrine, reproof, correction, and instruction in righteousness. And if I am able to judge, this is our most urgent need today.

This book is intended as a guide to the study of the Scripture text itself, not a substitute for it. Prepared originally for the training of young men entering the ministry, it has been reworked for the use of the layman in Sunday School and Bible Study groups. The writer has based his study on the original Greek text, but presents the results in a form suitable for those who will be using the English.

The discussion questions are intended for classes whose pace will permit their use. They are not offered to encourage the substitution of pious personal opinions for serious study of the Scriptures. They are intended to promote thought and lead to further investigation. All answers should be checked by the one all-important consideration: What does the Bible say?

The author wishes to acknowledge his gratitude for the help of several individuals who have contributed much to this volume: to Mrs. Irene Anderson and Miss Vicki Powers who did the typing; to Mr. Robert Ibach who prepared the maps, plans and charts; and to Dr. Herman A. Hoyt who read the manuscript, offered valuable suggestions, and wrote the Foreword.

CONTENTS

LIST OF ILLUSTRATIONS

FOR A WORLD
LIKE OURS

Studies in I Corinthians

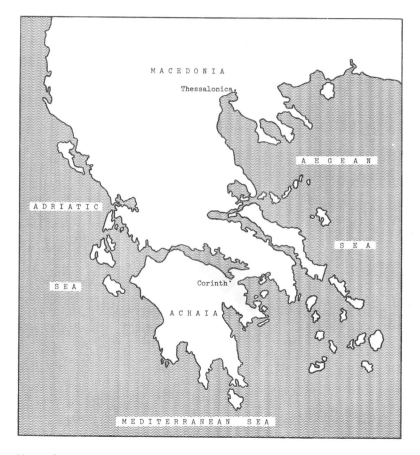

Map of Ancient Greece

INTRODUCTION

A CHURCH OF GOD IN CORINTH

I. THE CITY OF CORINTH

The land which we know as Greece is a mountainous arm thrust down into the Mediterranean between the Adriatic and the Aegean seas. The southern end of that land is almost completely severed from the mainland by a bay thrusting in from the west. Only a low, narrow isthmus about four miles wide saves it from being an island. Across the south end of the isthmus is a range of mountains, one peak of which, the Acrocorinth, towers over 1800 feet above sea level and 1500 feet above the low plain of the isthmus itself. On that plain at the foot of Acrocorinth was located one of the greatest cities of antiquity, Corinth. Archaeologists have found evidence of Neolithic and Chalcolithic occupation. Homer records that ships from Corinth were prominent in the siege of Troy. Its colonists established thriving centers of commerce in far-off Syracuse and Corcyra. It figured prominently along with Athens and Sparta in the Peloponnesian wars. It was the host and sponsor of the famous Isthmian games held every two years on the isthmus nearby and second only to the Olympic Festival. In New Testament times it was one of the chief commercial cities of the Roman Empire.

Its location made it a natural center of commerce and transportation. It had two ports, Cenchrea six miles to the east on the Aegean Sea (Rom. 16:1), and Lechaeum a little over two miles straight north, a port on the Corinthian Gulf which opened westward to the Adriatic Sea. Sailing in those days was hazardous, and rounding the southern tip of Greece was a perilous sea voyage, a detour of 200 miles. Strabo records the proverb, "When you round Malea forget your home." To avoid this, east-west-bound shipping between Rome and Asia used the isthmus at Corinth as a portage, unloading their cargoes and carrying them overland to be reloaded at the opposite port. They had even constructed a wooden slip-way by which they transported the smaller ships from one sea to the other. Pindar calls Corinth

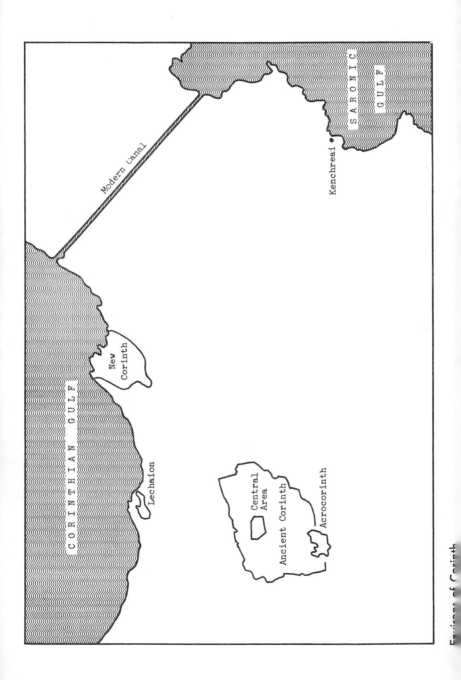

Environs of Corinth

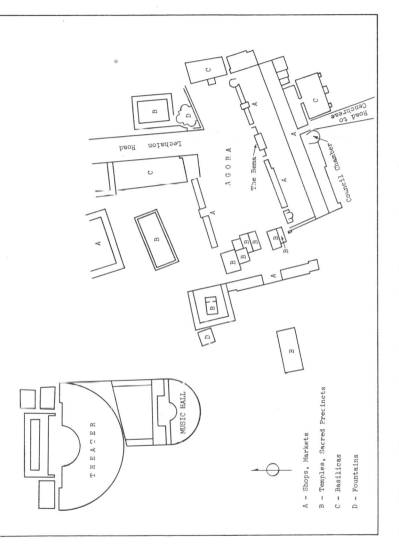

City of Corinth (Central Area) in the Time of Paul. Adapted from The Development of Ancient Corinth, by Henry S. Robinson (Athens: American School of Classical Studies, 1965, Fig. 7).

"the bridge of the seas." From earliest times it had been a maritime power. The first triremes were built there. It was also a gateway for all north-south routes between the Peloponnesus and mainland Greece. As a commercial center it was famous for its arts and crafts.

The ancient Greek Corinth was completely destroyed in 146 B.C. by the Roman general Mummius because it had taken the lead in an attempted revolt by the Greeks against the rising power of the Roman empire. At that time its art treasures and wealth were carried off to Rome, and were said to have equalled those from Athens. For almost 100 years the city lay in ruins, until in 44 B.C. Julius Caesar sent a colony of demobilized soldiers to rebuild it, making it the seat of the Roman province of Achaia. Almost immediately it assumed its former prominence as the richest and most powerful city of Greece.

Roman Corinth was built on the same site and after the same general pattern as its predecessor. It centered on an Agora, or market-place, a large open area surrounded by shops, temples, government offices, fountains, and so on. North from the Agora in a straight line stretched the road to Lechaeum. From the south side began the road which curved down to Cenchrea. It continued as a prominent city until captured by the Turks in 1458. In 1858 the city was destroyed by an earthquake and was not rebuilt, the survivors building a New Corinth on the Corinthian Gulf a few miles to the northeast. The ruins of the ancient city have been excavated by the American School of Classical Studies at Athens, beginning in 1896. A visitor to Corinth today sees the entire area of the Agora uncovered, with many of its surrounding buildings, and at a slight distance the theater and the music hall, seven pillars of an ancient temple of Apollo (the only remains of the old Greek Corinth) and a small museum. Perhaps most interesting to the Christian visitor is a large outdoor speaking platform located at about the center of the Agora, the "judgment seat" (Greek, *bēma*) of Acts 18:12-17, where Paul was tried before Gallio.

Corinth had two patron deities. Poseidon, god of the sea, was appropriately reflected in her maritime power and devotion to the sea. The other, Aphrodite, goddess of sexual love, was appropriately reflected in her reputation for immorality.[1] The cult of the goddess was perhaps more Phoenician than Greek, connected with the Astarte or Astaroth of the old fertility cult of the Canaanites. Her temple was located on the top of the Acropolis.[2] History records that it boasted a thousand female slaves, sacred prostitutes available to the people of the city and to its many visitors. Some of them were world-famous for their beauty and "attractiveness." Prices were high — they had a proverb, "Not every man can afford to go to Corinth!" — and their income was a major source of the city's revenues. This degrading practice, together with the looseness often characteristic of a port city of mixed and changing population, gave Corinth a reputation for wickedness far beyond the other great cities of her day. In fact, the Greeks invented a word, "to Corinthianize," which meant "to live an immoral life," "to have intercourse with prostitutes"; and "a Corinthian girl or virgin" was a synonym for a prostitute. Evidence of the accuracy of this reputation is seen in the New Testament, for it was at Corinth that Paul wrote the terrible description of pagan vice in Romans 1:18-32.

Corinth never was famous for its intellectual or philosophical accomplishments. It had no university and it never boasted any big-name philosophers. But it shared deeply in the innate Greek love for intellectualism, the craving to "tell, or to hear some new thing" (Acts 17:21). And judging from the contents of this epistle, this tendency among them was as productive of problems in the Corinthian church as was their background of immorality.

II. THE CHURCH AT CORINTH

Were it not that the power of the gospel makes such miracles

---

[1]One of the descriptive attributes of Aphrodite was *Pandēmus*, literally "belonging to all the people." The word was used in the sense of vulgar or common (cf. our word "promiscuous").

[2]The present writer has been unable to determine whether this temple on the Acrocorinth was rebuilt in the Corinth of Paul's time. But the Roman city, like its predecessor, was devoted by Julius Caesar to the same patron goddess — there was a temple to Aphrodite next to the Agora in the lower city — and evidence is clear that the later city even surpassed the former in its reputation for immorality.

commonplace, we could not but be amazed at the very existence of an assembly of God's saints in a place like Corinth. It began when Paul came to Athens and Corinth as a refuge from the opposition that had erupted to his ministry in Macedonia. On his second missionary journey he had received a call to "come over into Macedonia and help us" (Acts 16:9). In obedience to that call he had preached the gospel at Philippi, Thessalonica, and Berea. Intense opposition had arisen from the unbelieving Jews. Paul escaped to Athens, and a little later to Corinth. In these places Paul carried on a ministry, but apparently he was disheartened; his eyes were still northward to the Macedonian field, to which he was convinced the Lord had called him, and to which he had sent his helpers Silas and Timothy to assist the work and to bring word to him. His witness in the Jewish synagogue again brought opposition and blasphemy, so he turned to the Gentiles and continued his testimony in the home of Justus nearby. He needed encouragement and direction, and the Lord responded with a vision in the night encouraging him with the words, "I have much people in this city" (Acts 18:10). Taking this encouragement as a new *Corinthian* call, Paul settled down to eighteen months of missionary effort in the city of Corinth, a ministry rewarded by the establishing of a church there.

The Corinthian church was made up of some Jews, but mostly Gentiles (12:2). Most of the converts were from the lower classes (1:26), probably slaves and craftsmen. There were a few men of prominence. Crispus, the ruler of the synagogue, believed, perhaps precipitating Paul's ouster from the synagogue (Acts 18:8). Also, Erastus, the chamberlain (steward or manager) of the city, was among the believers who sent greetings when Paul later wrote his letter to the Romans from Corinth (Rom. 16:23). Some of the converts had come from lives of gross immorality (6:9-11).

After eighteen months Paul left Corinth to return to Judea and thence started his third missionary journey. In the meantime, a skilled and eloquent Jewish teacher from Alexandria, named Apollos, was brought to Christ and instructed in the Lord at Ephesus by Priscilla and Aquila. Moving on to Corinth, he was

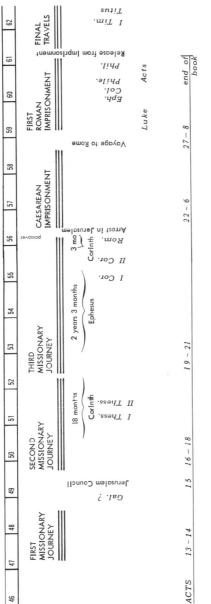

Chronological Chart of Paul's Ministry. Adapted from "New Testament Chronological Chart," by James L. Boyer (Winona Lake Indiana, Revised, 1962).

used mightily in the church there, and became their second great leader (Acts 18:24, 27; 19:1; I Cor. 3:4-6). Paul, on his third journey, arrived at Ephesus, just across the Aegean Sea from Corinth, and spent three years there. This great missionary had a real heart of concern for his churches, and from his nearby location he kept in touch with the Corinthians. It was inevitable that in such a church problems would arise. It was out of this combination of circumstances that the Corinthian correspondence came into existence.

III. THE OUTLINE OF THE BOOK

The outline proposed here is a structural one, based on suggestions found in the book itself. The basis is found in Paul's statements regarding the sources of information from which he learned about the situation at Corinth (cf. 1:11; 5:1; 7:1; 8:1; 12:1; 16:1). The topics dealt with are all "Problems in the Church."

    I. Problem Communicated by Personal Report (Chaps. 1-4).

   II. Problems Communicated by Common Rumor (Chaps. 5-6).

  III. Problems Communicated by Official Letter (Chaps. 7-16).

     1. Regarding Marriage (Chap. 7).

     2. Regarding Meat Offered to Idols (Chaps. 8-10).

     3. Regarding Church Order (Chap. 11).

     4. Regarding Spiritual Gifts (Chaps. 12-14).

     5. Regarding the Resurrection (Chap. 15).

     6. Regarding the Collection (Chap. 16).

Chapter 1

POLARIZATION AROUND PERSONS

(1:1-17)

I. EPISTOLARY INTRODUCTION

Letter writing was common in the days of the New Testament, and Paul follows the customary letter writing form of his day. But in Paul's use, each part of that customary form receives an amplification. These amplifications invariably reflect Paul's thought and feeling as he sets out to write; therefore, they foreshadow the contents and character of the letter which he writes and much profit may be gained by studying the particular statements made by the Apostle.

A. *The Signature* (v. 1)

First is the name of the author of the letter. "Paul, called *to be* an apostle of Jesus Christ." The words "to be" are italicized in the KJV[1] and are not in the original. Probably it would be better to omit them here and read simply, "a called apostle" or "an apostle by divine call." His apostleship was based not on his own choosing but "through the will of God."

The apostleship was a specific office in the early church associated with the work of founding the church (Eph. 2:20; I Cor. 3:10). Paul was expressing in these words his authority which authorized him to write such a letter as the one he is now beginning.

Paul associates with himself in the writing of this letter "Sosthenes *our* brother." Paul frequently associated another with himself in his letters. Usually it is Timothy, or Silvanus and Timothy. The reason for this association is not certain. Certainly it was not that they were joint composers or that Sosthenes was

---

[1]The King James Version of the Bible in English. Unless stated otherwise Scripture quotations will be given from it. This abbreviation will be used throughout when specific reference needs to be made to this version.

associated with Paul in a plural authorship. Probably, rather, he was someone well known to and respected by the Corinthian church and is mentioned as having been with Paul at the time of the writing and as giving his approval to the sending of such a letter. He is called "our brother," a term which shows that he was a Christian believer, one of "the brethren," a term frequently used for believers in the New Testament.

This Sosthenes may or may not be the same man as the one by that name mentioned in Acts 18:17. If he is the same, he has become converted. This would not be unusual, for his predecessor as ruler of the synagogue (notice v. 8) had been converted.

B. *The Address* (v. 2)

Paul identifies the ones to whom he is addressing this letter in three ways. (1) He addresses the letter to the church as a whole, the corporate body: "unto the church of God which is at Corinth," or, "unto God's assembly which meets in Corinth." The church is a called-out group, an assembly or congregation. To Greek Corinth the word would certainly bear the idea of an official body or assembly of citizens (cf. Acts 19:41). This is *God's* assembly, not of this or that leader, and the significance of this will come out as the chapter progresses. It should not be understood as a denominational name, although it has come to be one. The church is located "at Corinth," or better, "in Corinth." It is one center of the church of God, the one located in the city of Corinth. The expression involves in many ways a paradox, a miracle. God has a congregation even in wicked Corinth.

(2) The letter is addressed to the persons who make up the church individually, "to them that are sanctified in Christ Jesus." Note the change in number. There are *many* members in the *one* church. The word "sanctified" is in a tense which indicates the present state of sanctification resulting from a past experience of being sanctified. The word means to be set apart, or devoted to God; separated and belonging to God. Such is the past experience and the present state of all Christians. This is not a special elite group, or a second blessing which makes one perfect and sinless, as is very obvious when we look at the rest of the book which certainly does not reflect a perfect congregation.

Paul further identifies the members of this congregation by saying that they are "called *to be* saints." Again, the words "to be" are in italics and should better be omitted. They are saints by divine call, not a future expectation but a present position. The word "saint" comes from the same root as the word "sanctified" and is a further explanation of that term. It becomes the most common name in all the New Testament for believers, those who are saints.

(3) The Apostle Paul identifies the ones to whom he addresses the letter as including "all that in every place call upon the name of Jesus Christ our Lord, both theirs and ours." He thus broadens the address to include every believer of every age and place, even us who live in the twentieth century. This certainly suggests that the Apostle Paul was conscious of the fact that he was writing Scripture, not simply a letter which would be read and tossed aside, but one which would have permanent significance to God's people in every age. Certainly this is true of our age, when our world is so like his world. His term "those who call upon the name of Jesus Christ our Lord" was a common title in the early church for the Christian, the believer (cf. Acts 9:14, 21; 2:21). It is noteworthy that Paul uses the full title "The Lord Jesus Christ" six times in these first ten verses, a strong hint that something in the spiritual condition of this church at Corinth needed to be reminded of the Lordship of Jesus Christ.

C. *Salutation* (v. 3)

The third element in the introduction to a letter was the formal salutation or greeting, like our words, "Dear Sir." In Paul's day this was expressed customarily by using a form of the word "to rejoice" (Greek, *chairein*), meaning "I wish you well," "May you be glad," or simply, "Greetings." Among the Jews the customary greeting was, as it still is, the Hebrew word *Shalom*, "Peace." Paul combines these two, taking a related form of the Greek word (*charis*) with its fuller Christian connotation of "grace," and coupling it with the Hebrew greeting of peace, thus forming the usual pattern of greeting in most of the New Testament epistles, put in the form of a wish or a prayer, "May grace and peace be yours." Grace refers to the abundance of God's undeserved gifts and, therefore, an objective wish. Peace refers to the condition that results when God is related to us in grace and all is well between us, hence the subjective quality of peace. The Source and the Giver of these blessings is identified — "from God, our Father, and from the Lord Jesus Christ." Paul always gives Jesus a rank of equality with God, using a grammatical construction which makes Him parallel with God the Father.

D. *Thanksgiving* (vv. 4-9)

Another element in the introduction to ancient letters was an ascription of thanksgiving or appreciation, often addressed to the pagan deity, in which the writer of the letter finds some particular thing about the one to whom he writes for which he is grateful. The Apostle Paul also begins his letters with such a thanksgiving, in every instance except two. It is especially instructive to note what Paul sees in the Corinthian Christians which was worthy of thanksgiving.

1. *For Their Past Blessings* (vv. 4-6)

Paul thanks God (1) for their past bestowal of grace (v. 4). The verb is in the past tense and should be read, "for the grace of God which was given you in Jesus Christ." This is not a present continual bestowing but rather a past tense referring back to their experience of salvation, to their conversion. It was a bestowing of God's unmerited favor upon them and it came to them because they were in Christ Jesus.

Also, he thanks God (2) for their past enrichment by spiritual gifts (vv. 5, 7). The Corinthians had been blessed with an abundance of the charismatic gifts of the Spirit, those special miraculous gifts which the Spirit bestowed upon the church in that first century era. Again the verb is in the past tense: They "*were* enriched" with all these spiritual gifts. The gifts particularly named here are the gifts of utterance and of knowledge. Utterance is perhaps the objective gift of being able to speak the truth. They were able preachers of the Word. Knowledge then would be the subjective gift of being able to apprehend the truth. They were intelligent, understanding hearers. It is interesting that these two gifts are singled out for special mention, for these two seem to characterize the Corinthian church. They prided themselves on these, and these were the gifts which were sources of trouble in the church at Corinth because of their pride, as we will be seeing in dealing with Chapters 12 to 14. The order in which these two are mentioned is also significant. Normally, knowledge should precede utterance. Here, speech is given prominence and this, in itself, may reflect the spiritual condition of the Corinthians. The result of this enrichment was that they "come behind in no gift" (v. 7). There was no lack of gifts. They had them all.

Paul next thanks God (3) for the past confirmation which they had experienced (v. 6). At the time of Paul's preaching the testimony of Christ to them, they had it confirmed by demonstration of the Spirit and of power (cf. 2:4).

2. *For Their Hope of Future Blessings* (vv. 7-9)

This is expressed in three phrases. (1) "Waiting for the coming of our Lord Jesus Christ" (v. 7). It speaks of the hope that they had in view of the early return of their Lord. The word "waiting" expresses confident, eager expectation or anticipation. It implies faith, i.e., they believed the promise; hope, i.e., they looked for its fulfillment; and love, i.e., they earnestly desired it, they longed for it (cf. II Tim. 4:8).

(2) "Who shall also confirm you unto the end, . . . blameless in the day of our Lord Jesus Christ" (v. 8). To confirm means to establish or make strong. The expression "unto the end" may suggest a degree (i.e., to the utmost), or, a time reference, until the revelation that they were looking for took place. The word "blameless" is especially interesting. It is a legal term which meant literally, "not called in," not called into court, not to have a charge or accusation placed against them, "unaccused." It does not carry the sense of having no blame, or having no sin; but rather that there is no charge placed against them. This is the condition of one who is justified by his faith in the Lord Jesus Christ. There are no charges against him. This will be true as they look forward to it "in the day of our Lord Jesus Christ," the day when the Lord will appear and His saints will be revealed before the world.

(3) "God is faithful" (v. 9). Their calling was through God and He is faithful; therefore, their calling is sure. The strength of Paul's confidence in behalf of the Corinthian Christians was not because of their present condition, but because of God's faithfulness.

3. No Thanksgiving for the Present

Note that the Apostle Paul, contrary to his customary way in his other letters, has said nothing of their present condition in this thanksgiving. And the fact that he can find cause to give thanks to God only for their past and their future brings a serious implication of failure in their present spiritual condition.

II. FIRST PROBLEM: FACTIONS IN THE CHURCH

With verse 10 Paul begins his treatment of the first main division of his book, a discussion of the problem which had arisen through a contentious spirit in the church, which had produced a polarization around prominent persons. Paul's treatment of this problem occupies the first four chapters of his book. He begins by giving a general statement of the situation and makes some remarkable remonstrances on it (1:10-17). There follow two main arguments: first, against a wrong conception of the nature of the gospel (1:18—3:4; see chap. 2); and second, against a wrong conception of the ministry (3:5—4:21; see chap. 3).

A. An Exhortation (v. 10)

The exhortation contained in verse 10 implies the existence of divisions in the church. The words "I beseech you," should be understood as exhorting, urging, encouraging, rather than begging. Paul appeals to them as "brethren" (Paul doesn't sever relations with them because they have problems), and "by the name of," or through their relationship with the Lord Jesus Christ. The exhortation includes three things. (1) "That ye all speak the same thing." There is need for uniformity of testimony on the part of believers, and the word implies more than mere verbal agreement. It is not enough that they all should use the same words. Paul wants that they should *mean* the same thing as well, for the word that is used implies not so much the particular words that are used as the meaning or the significance of the words. (2) "That there be no divisions among you." The Greek word used here is related to our word "schism." Its root meaning is "to split" (cf. schizophrenia), and is used in Matthew 9:16 for a rent in a garment. It should be noticed that the Apostle Paul does not accuse the Corinthians of schism; he rather warns them that there should not be schism. There is a danger that schism may develop (cf. 11:18, where Paul expresses the fear that it has actually come to them already). (3) He admonishes them that they "be perfectly joined together." The Greek word here means literally "to put in good order," or "to restore." It is used in Matthew 4:21 for mending nets, and in Galatians 6:1 for restoring those who are caught in a fault. The Greeks used this word for the mending of broken bones. It is the exact word for the healing of the breaches caused by strife. Thus in this exhortation the Apostle Paul, while not actually charging that there were schisms within the church at Corinth, yet evidently implies that there were conditions prevalent there which were in danger of becoming schisms and which needed to be rectified in order that the believers might be joined together in the same mind and judgment.

B. *The Actual Charge* (v. 11)

Evidently, some of the household of Chloe had come from Corinth to Ephesus and had reported to the Apostle Paul the situation in the church at home. Who were these of Chloe? They are not known to us, but obviously they were well known to the Corinthians. This problem that Paul is dealing with was not a thing that was spread by gossip. Those who carried it were willing to be identified. Paul identifies the problem in specific details. "There are contentions among you." The word used here implies wrangling, strife in words, personal contentions, quarreling, bickering. In classical Greek it was sometimes used to mean rivalries. Thus, the charge that Paul brings against the Corinthian church is not that there were actual divisions present, but that there was a factious, contentious spirit being manifested which was in danger of bringing divisions in the church.

C. *A Detailed Explanation of the Charges* (v. 12)

Paul procedes to explain further what he means. "Now this I say" (v. 12), is the Greek way of saying, "This is what I mean" (cf. 10:29; Gal. 3:17; Matt. 26:70).

1. *Who Were Involved?*

"Every one of you saith." This expression is emphatic and it shows that these claims were being made by individuals. They were not well-defined parties in the church, but claims being made by various individuals in the church. And the expression makes it clear that all of them were involved. They were all taking sides and participating in the factions.

2. *The Claims Which Were Being Made*

These claims were being expressed in the words, "I am of Paul; and I of Apollos; and I of Cephas; and I of Christ." Or, as we might say it, "I am Paul's man," "I am Paul's follower," "I belong to Paul," and thus with the others.

Care is needed that we do not misrepresent the nature of these parties in the Corinthian church. They have been distorted out of all proportion by certain Bible critics who try to see in them a basic conflict in the early church between Peter and Paul, between the Jewish and the Gentile branches of the church. Needless to say, the terms that are used here give no support whatever to that notion. Nor are these parties to be understood as the originators of sects or denominations. In fact, these parties were evidently of short duration, for when Paul writes his second epistle to the Corinthians we find him dealing with many other problems which afflicted the church at Corinth, but there is no trace of any further consideration of this particular problem. Evidently, the divisive spirit there was effectively corrected by this letter from Paul and the factions did not develop any further. We should not think of these factions as being hard and fast, well-defined parties in the church at all. Rather these are individual claims and preferences, rivalries and bickerings among the members as to the leadership of certain popular leaders of the congregation. They were a reflection of one of the characteristics of the Greek mind, its love for wisdom and its enthusiasm

Synagogue Inscription. Fragment of lintel (?)-stone, bearing the Words, in Greek, [syna]goge Heb[raion], "Synagogue of the Hebrews." Photo by author.

for following the philosophical trends and patterns of the day (cf. Acts 17:21). That this is the case is shown clearly in the chapters that follow, when the Apostle answers the problem of the contentions in Corinth by a long discussion of the question of the wisdom of the gospel and its relationship to philosophy.

3. The Identity of These Parties

Two views are taken with regard to the identity of these parties. The first, the natural one, understands them to be just as they are described: people who were claiming to be followers of Paul, and of Apollos, and of Cephas, and of Christ. A second view has been suggested, based on 4:6, that Paul here arbitrarily substitutes his and Apollos' name for the real leaders to avoid embarrassment, and that the parties in the church at Corinth, therefore, were actually led by specific persons known to Paul but unknown to us, wholly unrelated to the names used. This writer prefers the first interpretation. Another explanation of 4:6 seems more natural.

Paul had preached at Corinth. A large number of the members of the church there were his converts, and it is not unlikely that many of them were very loyal to him. Apollos had been Paul's successor in the leadership of the church at Corinth. He possessed the Alexandrian culture and polished style characteristic of that school. He was a very effective expositor of the Scriptures (Acts 18:24, 28) and probably had a tremendous appeal to the philosophy-loving Greeks. Cephas, the Hebrew name for Peter,[2] probably was the leader being claimed by the Hebrew Christian element in the congregation, and this may hint at a Judaizing tendency in the church. However, there is no evidence that Peter himself was ever in Corinth. The Christ party may have been composed of those who recognized the errors of the other claims and assumed a superior title, claiming to repudiate all human leadership and to be followers of Christ himself. The very way that it is listed here, as one with the others, would indicate that they were doing it in a divisive spirit; disclaiming all human leadership and assuming a place of superiority or exclusiveness, a holier-than-thou attitude. In many respects this sectarian position is the most dangerous of all.

Obviously, the first two of these parties were the largest and the most influential. Paul deals with them exclusively in the rest of this epistle.

D. *Paul's Remonstrances against Such Contentions* (vv. 13-17)

Before he begins his actual developed arguments against them, Paul expresses himself in undisguised, surprised amazement, in a few rhetorical questions or exclamations[3] at the existence of such a situation.

---

[2]The name which the Apostle Paul always uses when he refers to Peter, except in Gal. 2:7, 8.

[3]There is some problem as to how these sentences should be punc-

1. *Is Christ Divided?*

Two views have been given of the meaning of this phrase: (1) that it refers to Christ's body, i.e., the church, in a dismembered state, and (2) that Christ himself is, as it were, cut up, distributed, and doled out in parts to the various groups. Either is possible. The latter seems to be more meaningful. It is more natural than to introduce the figurative reference to the church in this context, and it is more forceful and fully in accord with the mood of Paul's exclamation of amazement.

2. *Was Paul Crucified for You?*

This time the form of the question indicates that a negative answer is expected: "It isn't so, is it? Paul was not crucified for you, was he?" He wasn't asking the question in the sense that he was wanting an answer. He knew the answer. He knew that the mere asking would indicate their answer. Paul recoils with horror from the very suggestion that any Christian could say, "I am a follower of Paul."

3. *Were You Baptized into the Name of Paul?*

Again, it is a rhetorical question. The answer is obvious. The rite of baptism initiated them into the church. It was by baptism, spiritual and symbolic, that they all were united into one body, into the name of Christ, not of parties with men's names.

The introduction of baptism into this context indicates the important place which baptism occupied in Paul's thinking. In these three questions, the Apostle Paul reflects his initial reaction of abhorrence by appealing to three of the most important aspects of the Christian faith. Is Christ divided? This is an appeal to the *person* of Christ. Was Paul crucified for you? This is an appeal to the *cross* of Christ. Were you baptized into the name of

---

tuated. The KJV, the ASV (American Standard Version, Nelson, New York, 1901; this abbreviation will be used from now on), and many editors treat them as questions: "Is Christ divided?" The ASV margin and many other editors treat them as exclamations: "Then Christ is divided!" It seems that it really takes both of these to express the idea — "Is Christ divided?!" "Can it be?" It is both a puzzled question and a startled exclamation.

Paul? Here is an appeal to the doctrine of the *church* of Christ.
Paul introduces baptism along with, and parallel to, references
to the person and the cross of Christ, showing that baptism in
Paul's mind was important doctrine.

On the other hand, Paul emphasizes the unimportance of the
human agent in baptism. Verses 14 to 16 reflect this feeling. "I
thank God that I baptized none of you, but Crispus and Gaius."
This thanksgiving is a recognition of God's providential guidance
in his practice of baptism. He is thankful that God spared him
or safeguarded him against baptizing many. He mentions two:
Crispus, the converted ruler of the synagogue and perhaps Paul's
first convert in Corinth (Acts 18:8), and Gaius, Paul's host at
Corinth at a later date (Rom. 16:23). The providential reason
for this safeguarding was "lest any should say that I had baptized
in mine own name." Now, looking back on the situation, Paul
recognizes that it was of the Lord's guidance that he was safeguarded from a practice which might have brought misunderstanding.

Verse 16 introduces an interesting exception. Paul suddenly
remembers that there was another whom he had baptized,
Stephanas. From 16:15 and 17 we learn that Stephanas was
among those who had just arrived from Corinth and was probably present at the time Paul was dictating this letter. It may
well be that he prompted Paul, reminding him of the fact that he
had baptized him also, when Paul mentions the others. Now, if
Paul almost forgot Stephanas it might have been that he forgot
others also, so the Apostle Paul includes the possibility of others
as having been baptized by him. This does not argue against
the doctrine of inspiration. Inspiration did not interfere with
the personal style and characteristics of the individual writers,
nor did inspiration produce omniscience. Inspiration guaranteed
that what was written was what the Lord wanted written. Here,
the Holy Spirit inspired Paul to record his own forgetfulness, to
create the impression which He wanted, i.e., that the baptizer is
not important. That which is important in baptism is not the one
who does the baptizing, but the One into whom one is baptized,
i.e., into Christ, into the name of Christ. Paul's function in the
church was not baptizing but evangelizing (v. 17a). The expression here, of course, is not a denial that Christ commanded

baptism.[4] As apostle and missionary, Paul's function was evangelizing and establishing churches. He evidently baptized the first few converts until the church was organized and established; then the matter of baptizing was turned over to the local church and its officers, for baptism is a function of the local church.

The last part of verse 17 serves as a transition to the next great argument by introducing the mention of the gospel.

Questions for Discussion

1. Was this a real letter, or a religious tract in the guise of a letter? What are some of the marks of a true letter seen in the first chapter?

2. How does the Biblical use of the words "sanctified" and "saint" differ from the popular notion? Are *you* a saint?

3. When we want to thank God for our spiritual blessing, must we dig around in the dusty past or wistfully look away into the future? Or are we living in constant enjoyment of spiritual blessings today?

4. Is there room for differences of opinion among believers?

5. What is there in our present churches that reflects the party spirit of the Corinthians?

6. Is polarization around persons a serious problem in your church?

[4]That such is true is clear from the construction of the original. Paul uses the present infinitive, "not to be baptizing, but to be evangelizing." This is an explanation of a particular function and practice. Had he intended to deny that Christ commanded baptism he would have used the aorist infinitive.

Chapter 2

THE GOSPEL AND THE INTELLECTUAL

(1:18—3:4)

The Corinthian divisions evidently were judged by Paul to be basically related to their philosophy, their way of thinking. So when he begins his argument against this divisive spirit, he deals first with their false concept of the gospel. The key word in this next section is *wisdom* (mentioned twenty-one times; its opposite, *foolishness*, seven times). The transition verse (v. 17) which introduces this section uses the expression, "with wisdom of words." To the Greek mind it would suggest their love of intellectualism and their schools of philosophy. Evidently these divisions in the church were following the pattern of the Greek philosophers, with each following the leader he preferred and accepting his system. Such a concept of the gospel was making the cross "of none effect," emptying it of content, making it unreal. This section, therefore, is a rebuke of their intellectualism and pride of human wisdom.

I. THE FOOLISHNESS OF THE GOSPEL (1:18—2:5)

Later he will show that the gospel really is wisdom, but first Paul feels it necessary to point out in what sense the gospel is not wisdom, but rather foolishness.

A. *It Is Foolish in the Content of the Message* (1:18-25)

The foolishness of the gospel centers in its content; it is the preaching of the cross. Paul equates the preaching of the gospel (v. 17) with the preaching of the cross (v. 18).

There is a twofold evaluation of the cross message (v. 18). To some it is "foolishness." The word used here indicates stupidity or dullness (Greek, *mōria*). This evaluation of the cross is given by those who are perishing. The word "perish" does not indicate extinction, but ruin; not loss of *being*, but loss of *wellbeing*. The tense that is used indicates that the perishing is

34

already in process; those who are going in a pathway which leads to perishing. The opposite evaluation of the cross-message in this passage is "power." The vindication of the cross is not wisdom, that it *makes sense;* but power, it *works.* This evaluation to the cross-message comes from "those who are being saved." Again, the tense used indicates that they are in the process of being saved, salvation is going on.[1]

God's determined attitude toward wisdom is expressed in verses 19 to 21. In a series of quotations and illusions from the Old Testament, Paul expresses God's contempt for the worldly wisdom of the foolish; He will destroy, bring to nothing, make foolish the wisdom of this world. When it became clear that the world with all its wisdom had not come to know God, rather had turned aside from the true knowledge of God (cf. Rom. 1:21-24, 28), God determined by the foolishness of the message of the cross to save those who believe.

The expression "the foolishness of preaching" has often been misunderstood. It is not referring to the foolishness of the act of preaching, as a method. Preaching is not foolish as a method; actually it is very effective. Rather it refers to the *content* of the preaching. The word used (Greek, *kērygma*) means, not the act of preaching, but the thing preached, the message preached. God deliberately chose a message that was foolish to show His contempt for man's worldly wisdom.

The true content of the gospel message is again reviewed in verses 22 to 25, "But we preach Christ crucified." The message consists of a word about Christ, and a particular aspect of that word about Christ is that He is crucified. Note that it is not the preaching of the crucifixion, but the preaching of a crucified Christ, which constitutes the gospel, and it is precisely this which makes the gospel foolishness. To the Jews who want a "sign" (i.e., a demonstration, a proof of power) the cross is a

---

[1]It is interesting to note the tenses that are used in the New Testament for salvation. Romans 8:24 uses the aorist, or past tense, referring to our past experience of salvation at conversion. Ephesians 2:5 uses the perfect tense, referring to the present state of salvation which results from the past experience. Here, we have the present tense used, referring to the continuing process of salvation. In Rom. 5:9 the future tense is used, referring to the ultimate completion of salvation.

stumbling block, an offense. A crucified Messiah is a mark of weakness, not of power. To the Greeks, who want wisdom and philosophy (i.e., something sensible, something rational), the cross is foolishness. It doesn't make sense, it is stupid. It is like offering to a university group today some executed criminal as savior of the world. But to us, who are called from among both Jews and Gentiles, the crucified Christ is both. He is the power of God and the wisdom of God; wisdom because this message makes sense, and power because it works.

B. *It Is Foolish with Respect to the Recipients of the Message* (1:26-31)

In this section Paul shows that the gospel is foolish when judged on the basis of the type of people who receive it. He calls upon the church at Corinth to take a look at their membership list. "Not many wise . . . and mighty . . . and noble are called." The "wise" perhaps refers to the intellectuals, the educated class; the "mighty" to the important ruling class; and the "noble" to the respected aristocratic class in society. From this passage and many others in the New Testament it appears that with a few notable exceptions the vast majority of the converts to the Christian faith in the early church period were from the common or lower class of people. This fact is in accord with the sentiment expressed by our Lord in Matthew 11:25 and elsewhere. It is in sharp contrast, however, with the modern practice in church building, which often ignores the poor and lower classes and concentrates upon reaching the upper or better class of people on the theory that such will make for a more stable congregation.

Notice God's way of working (vv. 27-28). God loves to upset, to make ridiculous, man's pretenses of intellectuality. He does this by employing the foolish, the weak, the base things, the things that are despised, in order to bring to naught the things which are highly esteemed by man's wisdom. God's purpose in this (vv. 29-31) is twofold. (1) "That no flesh should glory," to shut off all human boasting. God hates pride and will not tolerate it. Every systematic theology that is based upon human philosophy has a built-in self-destruct device. (2) That all glorying may be in Christ. God has so arranged that all wisdom heads up in Christ (v. 30). He "is made unto us wisdom," and that wisdom expresses itself in and includes three things: "righteousness (i.e., past justification), sanctification (i.e., our present experience), and redemption (a word which is frequently applied especially to the future aspect of salvation; cf. Rom. 8:23).[2]

This reference to pride in human wisdom, which figures so prominently in this section of Paul's letter, must reflect something of the situation in Corinth and the reasoning back of the divisive spirit which existed there.

C. *It Is Foolish with Respect to the Minister, or the Preacher, of the Message* (2:1-5)

He next shows that the gospel has no claim to wisdom on the basis of the quality or importance of the one who did the preaching. Paul uses himself as an example. It was he who had brought the gospel to Corinth. That his preaching was not based upon intellectualism or worldly wisdom was manifested by his manner of speech (2:1), his narrow scope (2:2), his personal inadequacy (2:3), his method (2:4). Instead, he describes his method as being not by persuasion,[3] but rather by demonstration.[4] The success of the gospel in Corinth was not to be attributed to the persuasive methods Paul used: pleading, coaxing, "putting on

---

[2]This rather puzzling list of four qualities which Jesus Christ is to the believer is clarified by two considerations: (1) recognition of the fact that the term "redemption" is frequently applied especially to the future aspect of salvation (cf. Rom. 8:23; Eph. 1:14); and (2) the word order and connectives used in the original language. There it becomes clear that there are not four parallel words here, but rather one general, all-inclusive term, "wisdom," and three specific terms which describe that wisdom; namely, righteousness, sanctification, and redemption.

[3]"The spurious art of persuading without instructing, a contemptuous reference to the Rhetoric of the philosophers." G. G. Findlay, "I Corinthians," *The Expositor's Greek Testament,* Grand Rapids, Eerdmans, 1939, p. 776.

[4]"The technical term for a proof drawn from facts or documents, as opposed to theoretical reasoning; in common use by the Stoics in this sense." Findlay, p. 776.

the 'rousements,'" or his high pressure salesmanship. Rather it
was by the visible, real miracles of divine grace which God
worked and which were shown experimentally in the changed
lives of Corinthian believers. Paul's reason (2:5) for repudiating
the use of human persuasiveness in preaching the gospel was
to provide the proper foundation for their faith. The brilliance
of a great preacher is never an adequate foundation for faith.

II. THE WISDOM OF THE GOSPEL (2:6-16)

The contentious spirit which was being manifested in the
church at Corinth was due to a wrong conception of the gospel.
Evidently, they were thinking of the gospel as another of the
philosophical movements of the day and were comparing it and
its advocates with others as a type of rival philosophy. Paul has
made clear that the gospel is far from being another philosophy.
It is, in fact, foolishness. Now, however, he changes his approach.
Actually, the gospel is not foolish at all. It is wisdom, but an
entirely different kind of wisdom. He goes on to show in what
sense the gospel is wisdom.

A. *It Is Wisdom to Certain People*

The wisdom of the gospel is not apparent to everyone. Paul
has just shown that to the unbeliever, both Jew and Greek, it is
foolishness, and in 3:1 he will show that even to the carnal un-
developed believer he cannot speak as he would to the spiritual.
But here he describes the ones to whom the gospel is discernible
as wisdom: "them that are perfect" (v. 6). The word "perfect"
means "mature." It is not sinless perfection, or the arrival at ultimate perfection; rather it is the attainment of a mature or full-
grown stature (cf. I Cor. 14:20; Heb. 5:14; and its opposite in
I Cor. 3:1).

B. *It Is Wisdom in a Different Sense*

This wisdom is not the kind he has been speaking of in
preceding chapters. It is not of this age or its rulers (v. 6b).
He describes what kind of wisdom it is in verses 7 to 10.

1. *Its Origin* (v. 7). It is of God.

2. *Its Manner of Presentation* (v. 7).

This wisdom is described as consisting "in a mystery." The word refers, not to something which is mysterious or hard to understand, but rather something which is known only by revelation. A mystery is something that you cannot know until you are told. You cannot figure it out; it must be revealed to you. This mystery is one that has been hidden, unknown to the rulers of this age (vv. 7-9), but it has now been revealed to us. The channel of this revelation is God's Spirit (v. 10a). "To us" identifies the recipients of this revelation. These words in the Greek are emphatic, occupying the emphatic position at the beginning of the sentence. God has revealed them to us, in contrast with the rulers of this age who could not know them.[5]

3. *Its Prerequisite* (2:10-16)

Paul proceeds to explain the qualities or characteristics which make it possible for some to see the wisdom of the gospel when others are not able to see it. His discussion centers around the description of two kinds of men.

a. *The description of the spiritual man* (vv. 10-13, 15, 16). The spiritual man (1) receives revelation by the Spirit (vv. 10-12). Since only a man can understand the affairs of a man, so the Spirit of God (since He is God) knows and understands the things of God. Now Paul points out that we have received the Holy Spirit; therefore, we can comprehend spiritual things by the Spirit (v. 12). The possession of the Spirit of God makes it possible for the spiritual man to receive revelation from God.

The spiritual man (2) communicates spiritual things through the Spirit (v. 13). The means of communication is through "words," not those words which are taught by human intelligence

---

[5]Verses 9 and 10 present a problem of translation. In the original the quotation in verse 9 consists of a series of three clauses which do not constitute a complete sentence. Also, the better texts show verse 10 beginning not with the word "but" (as the KJV) but rather with the word "for." It is the preference of the present writer to take these words as a continuation of the thought begun in verse 7, resulting in the following translation: "but as it stands written, [we speak] things which eye has not seen, and ear has not heard, and has not entered

but such as are taught by the Holy Spirit.[6] The manner of communication is expressed in verse 13, "comparing spiritual things with spiritual" (KJV), or better, "combining spiritual thoughts with spiritual words" (NASB[7]), i.e., making the utterance correspond to the thought, using Spirit-taught words to express Spirit-given truth.[8] The spiritual man is thus able to communicate the spiritual truths which he has received from the Spirit of God to others who possess the Spirit, in words which the Spirit of God enables him to use.

The spiritual man (3) "examines all things"[9] (vv. 15-16). The Greek word used here (*anakrinō*) is a technical law term. It means "to make a preliminary examination," such as is the function of a grand jury. Ultimate judgment, of course, belongs to God; but the spiritual man is qualified to make preliminary examinations and to pass judgment with regard to spiritual truth.

It should be noted that these verses follow verse 14, the description of the natural man. Therefore, the contrast is obvious. The one who is not spiritual, by implication, is not even equipped to examine the evidence, let alone to pass judgment on a spiritual man.

-----

into man's heart; [we speak] things which God has prepared for those who love Him, for God has revealed them to us through His Spirit."

[6]This passage (v. 13) is often used to describe the inspiration of the Scriptures in the very words which the Holy Spirit teaches. Perhaps this is a true application but the context seems to make the basic teaching of the passage much wider. The "we" expressed here are those who have received the Spirit, and therefore refers not only to the apostles but to all mature Christians. Also, this "we" is contrasted with the natural or the unsaved person in verse 14. Therefore, what is said here of communicating with spiritual words must have its application to a broader scope than just the revelation of the words of Scripture.

[7]*New American Standard Bible: New Testament.* (Foundation Press, La Habra, California, 1963). This abbreviation will be used throughout.

[8]There are many other interpretations to this problematic phrase.

[9]ASV margin. It is the same word in the original as the last word of the preceding verse, "discerned"; a fact which is obscured in the KJV.

b. *The description of the natural man* (v. 14). Note, (1)
his limited nature. In contrast to the spiritual man, of whom
Paul has been speaking, this man is called "natural." The Greek
word is *psychikos*, "pertaining to the soul," and the word "soulical" has been coined to express in English the parallel between
this word and "spiritual." Just as the spiritual man is one who
is related to the Spirit and who lives in the realm of the Spirit,
so the "soulical" man is one who is related to the soul and lives
a life limited to the level of the soul. This word was first used
by Aristotle to distinguish the pleasures of the soul, i.e., ambi-
tion and desire for knowledge, from those of the body, which
were the grosser fleshly pleasures. Thus the word was used by
Greek writers to distinguish the noblest of men from the dis-
solute and pleasure-loving man who lives on the level of the
brute beast, the *akratēs* man. The natural man is the man com-
mended by philosophy, who is actuated by the higher thoughts
and aims of the natural life, not the sensual animal man who is
ruled by the passions of his body. This term therefore was
chosen by the Apostle Paul to describe to the Corinthians the unregenerate man at his very best, but a man who is limited to
the realm of the soul. His spirit, that part of him which is
capable of communion with God, is dead, unresponsive; it does
not function. Note, (2) his prejudiced disposition. He "receiv-
eth not [does not welcome] the things of the Spirit of God."
Note, (3) his distorted judgment. "They are foolishness unto
him." Note, (4) his inadequate abilities. "Neither can he know
them," or even more strongly, "He cannot even begin to know
them." He is a man who is limited to the senses. He lacks the
equipment necessary to examine spiritual things. The only ave-
nue of entrance to spiritual things is closed to him for "they are
spiritually discerned," and he does not have the Spirit. He is like
a blind man in an art gallery, like a deaf man at a symphony.

III. THE CARNALITY OF THE CORINTHIANS (3:1-4)

In the preceding section Paul has divided men into two classes,
the Natural Man and the Spiritual Man. But as a matter of fact,
when Paul came to speak of the Corinthian Christians he couldn't
treat them in either of these two groups. They were not spiritual

as described in the preceding verses. He said, "I could not speak unto you as unto spiritual." Neither were they natural. He uses the word "brethren" to describe them, a term which makes it plain that they were believers. He calls them "babes in Christ" and in fact they are among those addressed earlier in the epistle as "them that are sanctified." So to describe the Corinthians he creates a third category; an abnormal, unnatural one, one that shouldn't exist at all, and one that is the object of his criticism. He speaks of them as "carnal."

A. *They Were "Babes in Christ"*

The word "babes" is a reference to the new birth. Those who are born again enter into God's family and they begin that life as babes. This is a natural situation and there is no fault implied in the term, but the Corinthians had remained babies too long. "Neither yet now are ye able" (v. 2; cf. also Heb. 5:12-14; 6:1). Thus, the expression "babes in Christ" means that they were born but they had not grown up. The proof of this prolonged infancy is to be seen in their diet. "I have fed you with milk, not with meat" (v. 2). The plain, unmistakable point of the illustration, here as in the parallel Hebrews 5, makes it clear that "milk," refers to the simple, elemental truths of the gospel, "the first principles of the oracles of God" (Heb. 5:12), the foundation truths of repentence, faith, baptism, laying on of hands, resurrection, and judgment (Heb. 6:1-2). These are the ABC's of the gospel, the "Four Spiritual Laws," what is frequently, erroneously, called "gospel preaching."[10] Such a diet is fine for babies, but they ought to be growing up. The word "meat," of course,

---

[10]It is a commonly-held, but certainly unscriptural notion that the words "gospel," "preach the gospel," and "evangelist" in the New Testament refer especially to the initial presentation of the gospel for the purpose of bringing about a decision for Christ, the winning of souls, the initial experience of conversion. Instead, these terms are consistently used to refer to the whole good news of what Christ has done for us; including not only the initial experience of conversion, or justification, but also sanctification, Christian living, and even the hope of glorification in the future. Never are they used in the restricted sense of "getting folks saved," to the exclusion of God's continuing work in salvation.

refers to the deeper truths about Christ and the Christian life. In Hebrews 5:10 and 11 the context indicates that the "meat" refers to the discussion of the priesthood of Christ.

B. *They Were Carnal*

The word carnal means "fleshlike,"[11] displaying the character of one who lives after the old, sinful, fleshly ways. In Paul the flesh is often used as the opposite of the spirit. The Christian life is described as a conflict between the flesh and the spirit (Gal. 5:16-25). Hence, these Christians at Corinth are to be understood as those who are losing that conflict, allowing the flesh to dominate.

The proof of their carnality is in their actions (vv. 3-4). (1) Their divisiveness proves their carnality. Each of the words used here is listed in Galatians 5:20 as the works of the flesh. In contrast the mark of spirituality in a Christian is unity (cf. Eph. 4:2, 3). (2) Their likeness to the natural man proves their carnality; they "walk as men" (v. 3). The natural man, being dead in the realm of the spirit and not having the Spirit that is from God, lives on the level of the *psyche*, the soul. The tragedy of these Corinthians is that they have allowed the spirit to be overcome in their lives by the flesh, and are therefore living like natural, unsaved men. This is a tremendous challenge from the Apostle Paul to all Christians that their lives should be different.

It should be clearly understood that the Apostle Paul is not dividing men into three parallel classifications. There are *two*

---

[11]Actually there are two slightly different Greek words translated "carnal" in this passage. The first (*sarkinos,* with the adjective ending *-inos*) means "made of flesh," implying its nature and constitution. The second (*sarkikos,* with the adjective ending *-ikos*) means "related to, or like flesh," "fleshlike." The distinction may be seen by comparing our English adjectives "wooden," "made of wood," with "woody," "like wood"; or "leathern" and "leathery"; here, "fleshen" and "fleshy." Paul uses the expression *sarkinos,* "made of flesh," in verse 1, but he does not accuse the Corinthians of being "made of flesh." He says only that he must speak to them as he would to those who are "made of flesh." When he speaks directly of the Corinthians he uses the other word, *sarkikos,* "fleshy." They were actually "like flesh"; they acted like people who were living in the flesh.

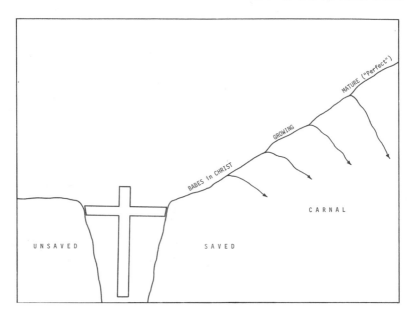

Classification of Men (I Cor. 2 and 3)

classes of men: the Natural, or unsaved man, and the Spiritual, or saved man. *All* Christians belong to the second group (cf. Rom. 8:9). But, because of the abnormal, unnatural situation existing at Corinth, Paul found it necessary to distinguish, within the group of those who are spiritual, two categories: (1) the mature ("perfect," 2:6), those who have attained the measure of maturity that is commensurate with their age, and (2) the carnal. Nor should "the carnal Christian" be considered as a necessary stage in the development of the believer. The normal progression anticipated here is from the natural man, through conversion, to a babe in Christ, then a normal growth toward maturity. The carnal state is a foreign state, one that should never be the experience of any child of God. It becomes a reality only when the believer gets out of the plan that God desires for him, fails to mature, and allows his former natural ways to dominate.

Questions for Discussion

1. Does the message of the cross make sense to today's intellectuals?

2. Are there groups today who are looking for "signs" or miracle proofs to support their religious convictions?

3. Does the gospel have more success with some classes of people than others? Why?

4. Are there methods of appeal in presenting the gospel which are unworthy or ineffective by Bible standards?

5. What is the essential difference between the natural and the spiritual man?

6. What distinguishes the carnal man from the spiritual? From the natural?

Chapter 3

THE ROLE OF THE MINISTER

(3:5—4:21)

Paul's second argument is that the factious spirit in the Corinthian church was based on a false concept of the ministry. They were thinking too highly of the human leaders, of Paul, of Apollos, and of Cephas. In this section of his letter, Paul seeks to correct their misconception by explaining the proper attitude toward God's ministers. "Who then is Paul, and who is Apollos . . . ?" (3:5). "Let a man so account [think, consider] of us, as of the ministers of Christ" (4:1).

I. HUMAN LEADERS ARE GOD'S WORKMEN (3:5-23)

A. *A Direct Statement* (v. 5)

Paul answers his own question by describing himself and Apollos as "ministers by whom ye believed." The word rendered "ministers" (KJV) here, is simply "servants" (NASB). It is the common word for service, for waiting upon someone to provide and care for them. It was used by Christ for His own service, and for ours (Matt. 20:28; Luke 22:27). It should not be given the official or professional connotation which frequently attends our use of the word when we speak of "the ministry." Paul and Apollos are simply servants, helpers, through whom they had become believers. And this was accomplished "as the Lord gave to every man" (better, "to each one," i.e., Paul and Apollos). Each was simply exercising the gift which had been supplied him by God's gracious bestowal. Thus Paul and Apollos, and all human leaders in the church, are to be thought of not as exalted leaders of factions, but as simple helpers exercising a God-given gift in leading men into faith in Jesus Christ.

B. *An Illustration from Farming* (vv. 6-9)

Verse 9 is a key verse showing the development of Paul's thought through this section. Note the change in pronouns, *"we* are God's fellow-workers.[1] *You* are God's husbandry, *you* are God's building." Paul and Apollos, and all human leaders, are God's workmen. The Corinthians are God's work, described by two figures: (1) "God's husbandry" (KJV), "God's field" (NASB). The word used indicates a cultivated field or land and therefore is approximately what we would express by the term "farm"; "you are God's farm." This is looking back to the illustration he has just been giving in verses 6 to 9. (2) They were "God's building," looking forward to the illustration to be given in verses 10 to 17.

The illustration from farming (vv. 6-9) affords Paul an opportunity to point out several truths about the proper function of God's servants (1) Different workers serve different functions (v. 6). Paul planted, Apollos watered. In both cases, of course, the result was God's work. (2) Various workers are of equal value, i.e., neither is anything. They both equal zero (v. 7). This, of course, doesn't mean that God does not use men or that they are not important. But in comparison with God, they sink into insignificance. The sentiment expressed here by the Apostle Paul is characteristic of his whole ministry (cf. II Cor. 12:11). Paul always magnified his office and glorified the ministry in the service for God. But he always minimized his own importance and gave all glory and credit to the God who enabled him to do his work. (3) Workers are not rivals; they are one (v. 8a). They are complementary, not competitive. The sower and the waterer are working together for a crop, for fruit.

[1]There are two possible ways to understand this interesting expression: (1) "workers together with God" (KJV); (2) "partners working together for God" (TEV; *Good News for Modern Man: The New Testament in Today's English Version,* American Bible Society, New York, 1966; this abbreviation will be used throughout). Apparently the language will permit either (cf. Wm. F. Arndt and F. Wilbur Gingrich, *A Greek-English Lexicon of the New Testament,* University of Chicago Press, Chicago, 1957). But the construction reflected in the KJV translation is a very rare one in Greek, and the context, at least so it seems to the present writer, favors the second rendering. Paul and Apollos are fellow workers with one another. They both belong to God. The emphatic word in each of these three clauses is "of God."

They have one aim and one purpose. They are not rivals working against each other. (4) Workers are distinct in responsibility and reward (v. 8b). The emphatic words here are "his own," occurring twice. Each worker has his own reward. The word used means "pay for work done." This is not a "reward" in the sense of a gracious gift, but "wages" for work that has been accomplished. This reward shall be "according to his own labor." The word used by Paul here makes it clear that the reward will be on the basis of the toil (Greek, *kopon*) or effort expended by the laboror, not on the basis of the amount of work (Greek, *ergon*) which he has accomplished.

C. *An Illustration from Building* (vv. 10-17)

Paul next illustrates the proper understanding of the function of the human leaders in the church by turning to the figure of a building. Paul and Apollos were God's workmen; the Corinthians were God's building. Just as workmen in the field are farmers so workmen on a building are builders. Human leaders are church builders. Paul uses this illustration to teach us what our attitude should be toward such workmen.

1. *The Foundation* (vv. 10-11)

The foundation, of course, is Christ (cf. Eph. 2:20; I Peter 2:6; quoted from Isa. 28:16). It is the "foundation of the apostles and prophets" in the sense that they laid it; they were the divinely appointed founders of the church.

2. *The Builders* (vv. 10-12)

Ultimately, Christ is the builder (cf. Matt. 16:18). Paul calls himself the master builder,[2] whose duty as apostle was to lay the foundation, get the work started. Next, "another buildeth thereon." In this context, which is dealing with a proper understanding of the work and function of the human leaders in the church, Paul must have in mind primarily Apollos and Cephas and other human leaders (v. 5). "We ministers are God's work-

---

[2]Greek, *architektōn,* not in the sense of "architect," the one who *plans* the building, but rather "the chief technician," the one who *builds* the building, what we might call the "general contractor."

men; you Corinthians are God's building, on which we are working." Thus, the main thrust of this illustration must be the function of the human leaders of the church, not a general function of all Christians.

However, there are several indications that Paul here intends to expand the application. Notice the indefinite and general terms he employs (v. 10, "another," "every man"; v. 11, "no man"; vv. 12, 14, 15, 17, "any man"). While the responsibility for church building is especially upon those whom God puts in the places of leadership it is also true that every member of the body has a part to contribute to the edification or building of the church (Eph. 4:16).

3. The Structure (vv. 9, 16, 17)

The building is made up of *people*. Verse 9 stated, "Ye are God's building." Verses 16 and 17 will re-emphasize it, "Ye are the temple of God." Ephesians 2:19-22 uses this same figure to describe the church and I Peter 2:5 speaks of believers as "living stones . . . built up a spiritual house." So the structure Paul is working on is composed of people, and his works which are to be tested are people (cf. 9:1). He is building a church by building people. It should be noted that the end and substance of a man's work for Christ must be men, people. Work has no value except as it relates to people.

4. The Building Materials (v. 12)

Six kinds of building material are listed. They obviously fall into two classes. The distinction is based (1) on permanence, their ability to stand a test to which they are to be subjected, the test of fire (v. 13), and (2) on quality or value. The wood, hay, and stubble are easily and cheaply acquired and used. They make a big showing fast. The gold, silver, and precious stones[3] are costly, less common, and involve more effort in their use.

---

[3]The material referred to by this term should be understood as marble or other building stones rather than diamonds, rubies, gems. This is indicated by their use as building material and by the fact that they appear third in a list which begins with gold and obviously follows a descending order of value (cf. I Kings 7:9-11).

What do these six kinds of building material represent? Certainly the context makes the primary application to *people*. They represent persons being built into the church. This is not to be understood, however, as a mere adding of another brick to the wall by getting another convert to Christ. Remember, these people are "living stones." They themselves grow, so that the temple grows and is edified as its people grow. Thus, the minister's work is twofold: He builds (1) by getting new people into the building, and (2) by getting those in the building to increase in stature and maturity. And since both of these tasks are accomplished by a ministry of teaching, there is some truth to the interpretation often encountered in the commentaries that the works here refer to the *doctrines* of the church leaders. Doctrine, however, is involved only secondarily, as it affects persons.

One should be warned, here, against the dangers of pressing this illustration too far. It is doubtful if the Apostle Paul intended that we should seek to find some spiritual significance in each of the six kinds of material named, or to get involved in such questions as whether gold, silver, and precious stones refer to saved people, while the wood, hay, and stubble refer to unsaved people, or whether the unsaved are built on the foundation of Christ, or whether the saved or unsaved are to be judged on the same day. This is to go far afield into imaginary questions which only obscure the clear force of the illustration.

5. *The Test* (v. 13)

The true evaluation of the work of each human leader is not yet clear. Paul thus implies a warning when he promises that the time will come when every man's work shall be made manifest. The factions in Corinth may have reason then to re-evaluate their estimation of their leaders. "The day" refers broadly to the day of judgment. Here, since the ones being judged are the believers, the reference must be the Day of Christ, i.e., the Rapture and the Judgment Seat of Christ (cf. 1:8, 4:5; II Cor. 5:10). "Fire" is simply a figure of speech for testing, for judgment, a figure which is appropriate to a building. This is a term which is widely found in the Scriptures (cf. Mal. 3:3, 4:1; II Thess. 1:8).

The Bema, or "Judgment Seat." A raised platform near the center of the market-place. Photo by author.

6. *The Outcome* (vv. 15-17)

The results of this testing are expressed in three parallel statements.

(1) If it endures the fire, he will receive reward (v. 14).

(2) If it is burned (v. 15) it will indicate of what sort the works were. He shall suffer a twofold loss: of the works themselves, and of the rewards that he might have had had his works been of a permanent nature. Yet he himself shall be saved. The builder here is evidently a saved person, and his salvation is not effected by his works, for salvation is by grace alone, apart from works. Yet, it is possible for a person to be saved — to get into

heaven, so to speak, as through fire — and to come through God's judgment of fire with nothing to show for his life's work except the fact that he is alive; like a man who loses all his possessions in a fire which destroys his home, and he is left with only his own life.

(3) If anyone defiles the temple (v. 17) he will be punished appropriately. The church, as God's temple is sacrosanct; it is inviolable. The word translated "defiled" does not refer to ceremonial defilement. It is never so used. Rather, it means either "to waste," "to damage," "to bring structural injury to," or "to corrupt morally," "to deprave" (cf. 15:33; II Cor. 11:3). God requites in kind. The one who destroys will be destroyed. The one who corrupts will be corrupted. This probably refers to an unsaved man,[4] to one who is not on the foundation at all, to the mere professor. While this letter and this illustration are addressed to Christian believers, yet it was being sent to an actual church which was composed of actual people, and there was always the possibility that within the ranks of the professing Christians there were some who were not actually born again. It is a bona fide warning to all that God will judge and destroy anyone who destroys or hurts the temple of God.

D. *Conclusion* (vv. 18-23)

Paul's conclusion to the argument of the section takes the form of a twofold admonition. (1) "Let no man deceive himself" (v. 18), addressed to those leaders involved, warning them against the pretense of wisdom; and (2) "Let no man glory in men" (v. 21), addressed to their followers. Do not glory in one leader. All of them belong to you; and you, in turn, belong to Christ.

---

[4]It should be kept clearly in mind that the judgment here involved is not to determine whether one is saved or lost. Salvation is *never* based on works; it is wholly a matter of grace, the gift of God by faith in Christ. Here Paul is dealing with a judgment based on works, and therefore has to do with rewards and punishments, not with destiny. Whether the man under consideration is saved or not is determined by his grace-relationship with Jesus Christ, but in *either* case his works will be judged and will receive their proper consequences.

II. HUMAN LEADERS ARE DIRECTLY RESPONSIBLE TO GOD ALONE (4:1-5)

Since human leaders are God's workmen doing the work He assigns to them, they are responsible to Him alone, and are therefore free from the judgment of men. The parties in Corinth were evidently evaluating their leaders according to their own likes and dislikes, and choosing between them on the basis of such judgments. This, Paul shows, is based on a wrong concept of the ministry.

A. *A Twofold Estimation* (v. 1)

"Let a man regard us in this manner" (NASB). The proper way to account of, or regard, or evaluate, human leaders is expressed in two terms. (1) "As of the ministers of Christ." The word used here (Greek, *hupēretēs*) had its origin in the Greek galley ships and originally referred to the "under-rowers." But it soon lost entirely its reference to the sea and ships and became a general term for any subordinate, an under-officer, an assistant, a helper. It was used of a physician's helper, of a king's retinue, of a synagogue attendant. Its counterpart in modern life would perhaps be a senate page, or an office boy, or a presidential advisor, or an assistant to the president (in distinction from a vice-president), or an assistant to a pastor. Paul uses the term to indicate that human leaders are assistants, under-officers, subordinates to Christ. They are not vice-Christs, substituting for Him when He is not around. Rather they are His personally selected errand-boys, standing at readiness to do His bidding. The use of this term makes it especially clear that Paul was thinking here of the personal responsibility of the minister to Christ and to Christ alone.

Human leaders are properly considered (2) as "stewards of the mysteries of God." The word "steward" (Greek, *oikonomos*) refers to a servant in charge of the affairs of the household and, therefore, the one who is responsible to the head of the house for the administering of his affairs. Its modern equivalent would be an administrator, an overseer, a trustee; that is, one who is responsible for the property, and desires, and instructions of another. The word "mystery" in the Bible denotes something which can be known only by revelation. It is not something that can be figured out from reason. It must be told. Christ's servants have been entrusted with a treasure of great truths, previously not known to men but now made known in the gospel. It is their responsibility to administer these treasures according to the instructions and the will of their giver, God. (For a similar idea, cf. Matt. 13:51, 52 and its preceding context.)

B. *A Twofold Implication* (vv. 2-5)

Such a description of the responsibilities of Christ's under-officers implies one supreme qualification — faithfulness; faithfulness to the responsibilities of the office, and more specifically, faithfulness to the interests of the Master. Other qualities may be desirable, such as ability, personality, imagination, tact; but above all else, when one is handling the property of another, faithfulness is required.

Another implication of this relationship, and the one which Paul is especially eager to express at this point, is freedom from human judgment (vv. 3-5). Paul applies this to himself and says, in effect, "It isn't important what you Corinthians think of me; it isn't important what men, in general, think of me; it isn't even important what I think of myself. In fact," Paul says, "I don't know of anything against myself, but even that is not what counts; I could be wrong. The one who rightfully is my only Judge is the Lord." He will judge in the light of all the facts. He will bring to light the hidden things and He will judge according to motives, according to the counsels of the heart (v. 5). His will be a proper appraisal and will result in praise from God. On the basis of this fact Paul exhorts the Corinthian factions, "Don't judge before the time," before the Lord comes (5a).

III. A PERSONAL APPEAL (4:6-21)

Paul's argument has been that divisiveness comes from a wrong attitude toward the ministry. Paul was one of those ministers. He closes now by an appeal to the attitude they had and should have toward him.

A. *His Reasons for Appealing to His Own Example* (v. 6)

Paul has been talking as if he and Apollos were leaders of these parties. That, of course, is not true. But these parties must have had actual leaders in Corinth, and Paul, to avoid offense, has deliberately transferred in figure his own and Apollos' name to enable him to speak freely of the matter. While these actual leaders are not named, they would surely get the point.

Paul had two lessons which he wished the factions in Corinth to learn from these matters. (1) They should not think too highly of men. How high is too high? Paul makes it crystal clear. "Not . . . above that which is written."[5] Paul's standard for what is proper, in this as in every other matter, is, "What does the Bible say? Don't go beyond what is written" (?) They should not "be puffed up for one against another." This is a reference to their party spirit. When they said, "I am of Paul" they were saying, in effect, "I am against Apollos." They were taking pride in being "for and against." There was really no basis for such, and Paul pricks the bubble of their pride by asking three pointed questions in verse 7.

B. *His Appeal to His Experience as an Apostle* (vv. 8-13)

How different are the arrogant, self-conceited pretensions of the Corinthians from Paul's experience as an apostle. The next section is a sadly ironic, almost sarcastic contrast between the pride of the Corinthians and the debasement of Paul. Perhaps a paraphrase of the passage will serve to bring out more vividly the thrust of Paul's words.

> [8]So you are already fully stuffed. You are so soon become wealthy and high class. You have been crowned as kings in the full enjoyment of your place in Christ's kingdom, and that in spite of the fact that we have not. Ah! That's fine! That's splendid! I only wish it were true, for then we too might be able to share in your exaltation. [9]But I am sorry to say that we poor apostles haven't gone that far yet; for apparently God has put us apostles at the end of your victory procession, like those who are under the death sentence, to show us off as spectacles of

---

[5]The Greek construction used here is incapable of literal translation into English and may be paraphrased, "Learn the meaning of the oft-quoted phrase, 'Not beyond what is written!'"

shame to the world and to angels and men. [10]Our profession of
Christ gets us branded as fools. For you, it means a reputation as
wise men. We are sickly, you are strong. You have respect and
honor, we have disgrace, contempt. [11]We go hungry and thirsty
and without clothes on our backs, are slapped in the face, without a home, [12]and we have to do manual labor. If anyone in-
sults us we smile back sweetly at them. [13]We are just the dirt
that decent people like you throw in the sewer.

Imagine how they must have felt when this was read before
their congregation at the next Sunday service! It was a bitter
medicine indeed, but one needed to cure their disease of pride.

C. *His Appeal to His Authority as Their Spiritual Father* (vv.
   14-21)

Tenderness follows sternness, and Paul lovingly directs their
self-accusations toward constructive ends. After all, he was their
father, their spiritual father; and as father he urges them to follow his example (vv. 16-17). But, also as father, he warns them
of impending discipline (vv. 18-21). He is planning to visit them
soon and he wants very much that his visit may be in love and
in meekness, not marred by a need to administer a spanking.
Which is to be is up to them.

Questions for Discussion

1. Is the ministry of the gospel an exalted profession? In
what sense? How does Paul speak elsewhere about his evaluation of the ministry?

2. Is there a place for rivalry and competition in the Lord's
work?

3. Are there times when property, or programs, get ahead
of people in the church's priorities? Discuss some specific instances.

4. Will Christians who get into heaven "so as through fire"
with their works destroyed, be happy there? Is it right to be
concerned about our reward for faithful service?

5. When Paul insists that God's ministers are responsible to
Him alone, does this give them dictatorial powers over the
church?

6. How much authority does a minister have?

Chapter 4

PURGING THE IMPURE

(5:1-13)

Here Paul turns to the second problem which he is to deal with in his epistle. This one, along with those in Chapters 6 and 7, belong to the category of moral problems. It concerns a notorious case of immorality in the Corinthian church.

Paul probably learned of it by way of gossip or common rumor, as expressed by the KJV and most translations and commentators,[1] Paul was in Ephesus, across the sea and far removed from the Corinthian community, yet the situation was so bad that rumor had reached even to this far-off place. He certainly would have consulted or checked with those from Corinth who were present with him in Ephesus and satisfied himself regarding the facts. Actually the nature of the situation was such that the facts were obvious. There were no extenuating circumstances or consideration of motives that could change the sinfulness of this situation. You do not need a church trial to determine when a man is married to his stepmother. Hence, Paul's words and actions with regard to this situation are not dependent on hearsay alone. The fact that he has heard it from gossip or rumor actually makes the case stronger. It was such a flagrant case of sin that everybody knew about it.

It is a great mistake to think of this chapter solely as a condemnation of fornication, addressed to the guilty man. Rather, this is addressed to the church, and shows Paul's greatest concern to be the sinful attitude and state of the congregation, and its rectification. Actually, he deals with both.

---

[1] R. C. H. Lenski, *The Interpretation of St. Paul's First and Second Epistle to the Corinthians* (Wartburg Press, Columbus, 1957, p. 206) suggests that the meaning is: Fornication is heard of among them; among them the report is common; implying that those who know it by rumor are in Corinth. If so, Paul must have gotten the information from "those of Chloe" (1:11) or from Stephanas and his friends (16:17).

I. THE TWOFOLD SIN (5:1-2)

A. *The Sin of the Man* (v. 1)

The specific sin involved here is a particularly shameful case of incest (marriage within the circle of close relatives). The man is not named. He was evidently a member of the congregation, a professing Christian (v. 12). For the same reason it is evident that the woman was not a member of the congregation; no word of blame or judgment is addressed to her. Probably we are to understand that she was his stepmother, rather than his mother.[2] The expression, "his father's wife," is taken from the Mosaic law (Lev. 18:8; Deut. 22:30).[3] The father, of course, is not mentioned here.[4] It is unknown whether he is dead, or whether he is divorced from his wife, or still legally related to her. None of these situations would effect the heinousness of the crime involved.

The relationship involved is seen in the expression, "that one should have" (Greek, *echein*). The tense used implies a continuing relationship. The word used implies some official relationship. It is used in Greek generally and in the New Testament particularly to refer to the marriage relation (cf. John 4:17; I Cor. 7:2, 12-13, 29; Gal. 4:27). Many commentators claim that the words mean they were married. Others refer to some kind of permanent concubinage. The least that can be said is that they were living together as man and wife. This was far more than just having an affair with his father's wife. They were openly and obviously in the sight of the whole community living together as man and wife. The term "fornication" is a general term for sexual immorality. The enormity of the sin is emphasized by Paul's statement that such was not even tolerated by

---

[2]The words, of course, could mean either. The probability is based upon the degree of indecency we are prepared to expect.

[3]Other passages dealing with this same subject are I Chron. 5:1 (cf. Gen. 35:22); II Sam. 16:22; and Amos 2:7.

[4]Many have seen this case of immorality as constituting the background of Paul's reference in II Cor. 7:12. If this is the case, and the present writer believes that it is very unlikely, then it would imply that the father was living and probably that he was a Christian.

heathen standards.[5] Low, indeed, were the moral principles of the heathen world and mere fornication was excused and often approved, but even they stamped this sin with infamy. But Paul goes further in emphasizing the terribleness of this sin. In verse 3 he speaks of "him that hath *so* done this deed." This word "so" is emphatic in the Greek and draws attention to the brazen attitude or manner in which the deed had been done.

B. *The Sin of the Church* (v. 2)

It is against the church itself that Paul launches his sternest rebuke. They are guilty of two sins.

1. *The Sin of Pride*

Of course, he is not saying that they are puffed up over this, as if they were actually boasting of the sin. Rather they are puffed up in spite of it. This sinful condition is present and they are still puffed up. The Corinthians were proud and boastful of their wisdom, their knowledge, their utterance, their spiritual gifts, and so on, and even this terrible situation had not punctured their pride. Their self-conceit lay at the root of this shameful situation, just as it was the basis of their divided, factious spirit (chaps. 1-3). As W. E. Vine thoughtfully remarks, "Their self-complacency and pride rendered them insensible both to the scandal created among the outsiders and to the damage done to the whole assembly . . . A Laodicean spirit of self-satisfaction (Rev. 3:17) is responsible for manifold evils in an assembly."[6]

2. *The Sin of Impenitence and Callousness*

The normal and proper reaction of a congregation of God's people to such a shamefully immoral situation would have been shame and sorrow. They would have mourned as for the dead. But they had not done so, nor had they taken any action "that he might be taken away from among you," thus revealing that they had no real feeling of shame. They were callous and impenitent.

---

[5]Evidence for this may be seen in Findlay, *Expositor's Greek*, p. 807.

[6]*I Corinthians*, Oliphants Ltd., London, 1951, p. 71.

II. THE TWOFOLD ADMONITION OR CORRECTIVE (vv. 3-8)

A. *For the Sin of the Man: Excommunication* (vv. 3-5)

For Paul there is no question about what should be done with the guilty party. Although he is absent, he sees clearly and has already judged what the action should be. The heavy and solemn language of verses 4 and 5 expresses its content. Carefully and with lawyer-like precision he gives his judgment.

1. *The Authority of the Action*

Four phrases stand out in verse 4 but their relationship to each other is not completely clear. Perhaps it is best to take the first, "in the name of our Lord Jesus Christ," as the basic authority for the action. Then the three remaining phrases list the various groups whose action is to be combined. (1) "When you are gathered together." The word used indicates an officially assembled congregation, what we might call an officially called business meeting. (2) "And my spirit." Paul, although not present in body, yet is very much present at that official business meeting by virtue of his expressed judgment recorded in this epistle and officially laid before their meeting. His spirit and advice would be powerfully present even though he, himself, were absent. (3) "With the power of our Lord Jesus Christ." Present also at that official gathering must be the recognized authority of the Lord Jesus Christ, the head of the church. Thus, authority to take disciplinary action against a wayward member must rest on the authority of the Lord Jesus Christ himself, and is to be exercised in an officially called congregational meeting at which there is present the voice of the apostle through the Word of God, and the conscious presence of the Lord Jesus Christ himself as head of the church.

2. *The Nature of the Action* (v. 5)

Whatever else may be involved, at least the action recommended here involved excommunication or expulsion from the church (cf. vv. 2, 13). But the expression in verse 5, "to deliver unto Satan," is an unusual one if it means only excommunication, and many have seen a further significance in it. Two interpretations are possible. (1) It is simply a term for excommunication. Since Satan rules in the sphere outside the church, so to be delivered unto Satan is to be put out of the church into the sphere where Satan rules. (2) It involves also a miraculous infliction of some physical sickness or affliction. The further description, "for the destruction of the flesh," has lent weight to this suggestion. Physical maladies are often ascribed to Satan, and spiritual benefits of such maladies are sometimes spoken of. It is known, of course, that the apostles had power to pronounce penal sentences in the physical sphere (e.g., Ananias and Sapphira, Acts 5:1-11, and Elymas, Acts 13:8-12). On the other hand, what is recommended here is not an apostolic action but a church action. If this is to be the action of the church, it seems it should be understood as referring to something that is available to the church today, rather than to the miraculous powers of the apostolic age. Perhaps the first explanation is simpler.

3. The Purpose of the Action: The Salvation of the Offender

The intended result of the drastic action recommended was twofold: the ruin of the flesh, and the salvation of the spirit. "The flesh," the realm in which the man was sinning, means more than the body. It refers, in Paul's usual sense, to the old man, the old nature, the lower element in mankind. Thus, sin destroys itself and ultimately brings the flesh to bankruptcy. The spirit, as opposed to the flesh, refers to the higher nature of man. Perhaps as sin brings about the ruin of the flesh, the man may be awakened to its futility and thus brought to realize the supreme importance of spiritual things; thus he will be influenced to turn to Christ and repentance. As Lenski says, "The expelled sinner takes with him the memory of Christ, of the gospel, of the church, and so on. When his flesh has brought him low, this memory may yet succeed in saving him."[7]

Thus the expectation and purpose of excommunication is the salvation of the offender. How different this is from the notion of some that excommunication is a consigning of an unrepentant

---

[7]*Corinthians,* p. 218.

sinner to a place outside the reach of the means of grace, and thus to everlasting doom and destruction.

Was this man in Corinth a Christian, a believer, a born-again man? The natural implication, I believe, is that he was not. This seems to be implied in the expression, "that the spirit may be saved." Also, verse 8 speaks of "the unleavened bread of sincerity and truth," perhaps implying that the sin of this man was insincerity and falseness. And in verse 11 Paul admonishes them, "If any man that is called a brother be a fornicator. . . ." The words "called a brother" would suggest that he was a brother only in pretense, not really one. However, if we believe it is possible for a born-again Christian to fall into so sinful a condition, then excommunication is still the solution, and its purpose is still his spiritual good, his salvation.

B. *For the Sin of the Church: Purging* (vv. 6-8)

With regard to their sin of pride, Paul says, "Your boasting is not good." The Greek word makes it clear that he is not speaking of the *act* of boasting but the *content* of their boasting. It is not that they should not be boasting, but rather that they have nothing to boast about. They were boasting about their wisdom, their knowledge (cf. chaps. 1-4). Now Paul says, "Know ye not?" Their knowledge was not anything to brag about if they did not know this.

With regard to their sin of callousness, Paul warns them of the seriousness of their sin and admonishes them to get rid of it. In doing so, he uses the symbolism of an Old Testament Jewish practice — the Passover and the Feast of Unleavened Bread. It was not that the Christians were continuing these rites or that he was admonishing them to do so; rather Paul, like the writer of the Epistle to the Hebrews, saw in many of these Old Testament practices a symbolic typology which pointed to Christ and the things of salvation. He saw the passover lamb as a picture prefiguring Christ, our Passover, who was sacrificed for us to bring about our deliverance from sin. Here Paul draws a lesson from the Feast of Unleavened Bread which followed the observance of Passover. For seven days after Passover the Jews ate no leavened bread. Their law required that they remove all leaven from the household, and Jewish sources furnish us with descriptions of the meticulous search which was made (___ house to guarantee their fulfillment of this requirement of unleavened bread. To a Jew it was unthinkable to observe Passover with leaven present. Now, just as Passover, with the death of the Passover lamb, speaks of the atoning death of Christ and our conversion through faith in Him, so the Feast of Unleavened Bread typifies the Christian life which follows conversion. The Christian life, Paul is saying, therefore should be one without leaven. Leaven, whenever it is used figuratively in the Bible, is a symbol of evil, of sin. So it is here. "Know ye not that a little leaven leaveneth the whole lump?" The statement calls attention to the contagious nature of evil. It is like one rotten apple in a barrel of good ones (imagine one good apple in a barrel of rotten ones!). In verse 7 he admonishes them to "purge out therefore the old leaven." Verse 8 specifies what he means, "the leaven of malice and wickedness." As it was unthinkable for a Jew to keep Passover without observing the Feast of Unleavened Bread, so it is unthinkable for a Christian to claim Christ as his Saviour from sin and to go on living in sin. The application is clear. "Purge out therefore the old leaven, that ye may be a new lump, as ye are unleavened."

III. A NECESSARY EXPLANATION (vv. 9-13)

A. *A Former Letter Misunderstood* (vv. 9-10)

It is clearly stated here that Paul had written another letter to the Corinthians, earlier than our I Corinthians. All that can be known about such a letter must be deduced from what is said here.[8] In it Paul had told them not to company with fornicators (v. 9). The verb is a double compound and means "to mix up with," or "to mingle with." Usage associates it with social inter-

---

[8]The opinion expressed by some that this earlier letter is to be identified with a portion of our II Corinthians must be rejected for at least two reasons: (1) Evidences for the unity of II Cor. (cf. the introductions to that book), and (2) the obvious fact that no part of II Cor. fits the description here given by Paul of the contents of that first epistle.

relationships. It is found only here (vv. 9, 11) and in II Thessalonians 3:14. The last passage makes it clear that it did not involve complete separation. Paul's admonition had said, "Do not associate with fornicators." But the Corinthians had obviously misunderstood his instruction. They had taken him to mean that they should have no association with the fornicators and the wicked men of the *world*. Evidently they had found this an impossible assignment and therefore had simply ignored it, paying no attention at all to Paul's admonition.

B. A Further Clarification (v. 11)

This time Paul makes crystal clear what he had meant. He did not mean absolutely or completely with respect to sinners of the world. He did mean absolutely with respect to professing Christians who were sinners. This time he adds the all-important qualifying words, "If a man that is called a brother be a fornicator, . . ."[9] The important word here is "brother," another New Testament designation for a believer, a brother in Christ, another son in the family of God. Even in that day such a relationship could be claimed falsely, the name assumed without the spiritual relationship. But Paul is not trying to differentiate. His term includes both the genuine and professing. The treatment he here advocates is to be applied to the Christian brother, rather than to the outsider in the world.

What is the precise nature of the discipline here demanded? The instructions are hardly explicit enough to become the basis of a legalistic, required procedure. The principle, however, is clear. The tense used indicates a continuing relationship. They were not to continue in social fellowship with the offender. But the treatment is to be severe and absolute, even to the point of refusing to continue eating with him. If an offending Christian brother should be subjected to this treatment, so cut off from all ordinary social fellowship with his Christian brothers even to the extent that they refuse to eat with him, that would exert tremendous pressure on him to amend his ways.

[9]"With any so-called brother" (NASB), "professing Christian" (J. B. Phillips, *The New Testament in Modern English*, Geoffrey Bks., London, 1960).

What sins are to be subject to such treatment? Six offenses are listed here (v. 11). Perhaps this is not to be considered as a complete list, for he enlarges it by adding four more in 6:9-10. Certainly an unrepentant continuance in any of these sins would be grounds for such excommunication. (1) A fornicator is one guilty of any sexual immorality. (2) The covetous is a greedy, grasping person, one who is always after more. This sin will be the special subject of consideration in the next chapter. (3) The idolator can hardly be an open pagan since he is called a brother. Possibly he is a Christian who still participates in heathen feasts (cf. 8:7-10; 10:20-21). Or perhaps, in accordance with Colossians 3:5, idolatry is to be defined as covetousness. Strange as it may sound to our ears, idolatry was a sin which was possible even to professing Christians (cf. I John 5.21). (4) The railer is the reviler, one who speaks harshly, reproachfully, uses abusive language. The offense of (5) the drunkard is obvious. (6) Extortioner comes from the root meaning "to seize by force," "to plunder"; hence, a robber. Or perhaps the meaning here is "swindler."[10] Such a list surprises us when it is associated with professing Christians. But history and experience warns us against being too confident. These are not the only sins nor indeed the worst sins possible to Christians. But they are the open, obvious sins which deserve to be dealt with in open, obvious treatment by excommunication and the infliction of social ostracism.

C. *A Simple Explanation and Application* (vv. 12-13)

Perhaps we are a bit startled by the action which Paul advocates here, that we treat sinning brothers more severely than we do sinners out in the world. He closes this section by explaining why. Judging the outsider is God's responsibility, not ours. Judging the insiders is as far as our responsibility goes. And that responsibility is clear. In the particular instance before the church at Corinth, the incestuous man, Paul states his conclusion: Put him away.

---

[10]Adolf Diessmann, *Light from the Ancient East*, Doran, New York, 1927, p. 317, p. 316, note 6.

Questions for Discussion

1. Should rumor or gossip be heeded?

2. Is gross immorality a problem in today's churches?

3. Should church discipline be used more? In what cases? Of what should it consist?

4. How do you purge sin from a congregation? From an individual's life?

5. Why should we be more strict about associating with sinning Christians than with sinning unbelievers? Is this a double standard?

6. What does the admonition not to eat with the sinning brother involve? Does it refer to the Lord's Supper? to Sunday School class meetings? to business lunches? to the family table?

Chapter 5

MONEY AND MORALITY

(6:1-20)

The very location of this incident is instructive. It deals with law-suits, business matters, property, money — and Paul places it in the midst of a section which is dealing with gross immoralities. Note the order: (1) the incestuous man (5:1-8), (2) admonition to separate from all immoral persons within the church (5:9-13), (3) this section on law-suits, (4) list of immoralities which shut one out of the kingdom of God (6:9-11), (5) Christian liberty and licentiousness (6:12-20), and (6) instructions regarding marriage in a context of fornication (ch. 7). There is no real break in the context through Chapters 5 and 6, and by implication this also is a moral problem (cf. the inclusion of covetousness among the lists of sins in 5:10, 11; 6:9, 10). The sins of impurity and covetousness are kindred sins. Both were prevalent at Corinth, both are destructive of society, both are basically selfishness, and the lamentable lack of church discipline in Corinth allowed both to flourish.

I. BROTHER AGAINST BROTHER IN COURT (6:1-11)

A. *The Nature of This Problem*

The occasion for this section of the epistle was the fact that in Corinth Christian brethren were taking their differences with each other into the secular courts instead of handling them between themselves as brethren. And these differences were not of a spiritual or religious nature. The word Paul uses twice (Greek, *biōtika*) indicates matters pertaining to one's livelihood, to secular matters: money, property, and so on ("matters of business disputes," NEB[1]). This, then, furnishes an illustration of the second, i.e., covetousness, in the list of immoralities which Paul has just given.

---

[1]*The New English Bible: New Testament.* Oxford, 1961. This abbreviation will be used throughout.

B. *The Seriousness of the Problem* (vv. 1-3)

There are two indications of how Paul looked at this matter. (1) These Corinthian Christians were showing an unholy audacity and insolence, as expressed by the word "dare" (v. 1). (2) They were showing an ignorance of scriptural truth (vv. 2, 3). Three times in this section the expression occurs, "Do you not know?" (vv. 2, 3, 9). In spite of their prided knowledge, the Corinthians evidently were ignorant of some of the simplest truths. (a) That the "saints will judge the world" (v. 2) had been taught in the Old Testament (cf. Dan. 7:22) and is also in the New (cf. Rev. 20:4; 2:26-27; 3:23; also Matt. 19:28 and other passages where the saints are said to "reign"). (b) That the "saints will judge angels" (v. 3) is nowhere else taught specifically. Perhaps it is implied generally in the fact that the saints are to be associated with Christ in judgment. It certainly is taught clearly here, and that is enough to establish it as a scriptural truth, although it does not explain why the Corinthians should have known this truth. We probably should understand that the Apostle Paul had taught this truth when he was with them. (c) By an easy deduction, arguing from the greater to the lesser, saints ought to be able to judge these smaller matters.

C. *The Twofold Sin Involved* (vv. 4-8)

1. *Going before the Secular Courts* (vv. 4-6)

On the surface at least, the sin which Paul is referring to is the impropriety of trying to settle their differences before outsiders. They should have been able to settle their disagreements within themselves. Even the least Christian should be able to handle these matters (v. 4).[2] "Shame on you!" (v. 5), Paul writes.

---

[2]Two interpretations are possible for verse 4. One takes it as a question: "Do you appoint them as judges who are of no account in the church?" (NASB), i.e., the unbeliever. The other takes it as a command given in irony: "Pick the poorest excuse you have got as a Christian and set him as your judge in such matters! Surely he is competent, since you are all going to judge the world and angels!" (My paraphrase.) This is probably the meaning intended by the KJV.

Julian Basilica: Detail of Roman Law Court (First Century A.D.). Levant Photo Service.

It should be carefully noted that Paul does not belittle the secular courts here. There is not a word of criticism or disrespect for the courts of the land. On other occasions Paul himself had appeared before these courts, and on several occasions was benefited by them. What he is condemning here is the practice of Christians taking Christians before secular or outside courts. Human courts have their place and serve a useful function in human society. But certainly Christians, who constitute, as it were, a society of judges, have no need for them.

2. *Going to Court at All* (vv. 7-8)

It is quite obvious that Paul is charging the Corinthians with more than merely the fault of going before secular courts. There is a far more serious moral deficiency evidenced by their actions. It is their disposition to demand their rights rather than to practice the Christian virtue of self-denial and non-resistance.

Verse 7 admits two interpretations. (1) It is wrong; it is a fault (KJV) to go to law with one another. (2) It is already a defeat for you that you have law-suits with one another (cf. NASB), taking the expression as a technical phrase meaning "to lose one's case." The meaning is, "You've lost your case before you even get to court. Even if you win the decision you are still a loser because you have lost your brother's fellowship and respect. You have lost your testimony before that brother and others who know of the situation." Either of these interpretations makes good sense. The latter appears to be the more forceful.

The latter part of verse 7 expresses what Paul feels they should have done. Rather than go before heathen courts, rather than even set up Christian courts to handle the matter, they ought to have submitted to injustice, to have ignored their rights, to have allowed themselves to be defrauded. It is clear from this that the Apostle Paul took seriously the teachings of our Lord Jesus Christ concerning non-retaliation and non-resistance (Matt. 5:38-42; Rom. 12:19 offers further evidence). What Paul is saying is, "Even if you are right, you are wrong to claim your rights." This is not an easy doctrine to accept, nor is it a popular one. But it is unquestionably the teaching of our Lord and the teaching of Paul; in fact, it is the teaching of the New Testament.

Instead of this proper Christian reaction, Paul charges that the Corinthians were actually trying in turn, by going to court, to wrong and to rob the ones whom they claimed were trying to rob them (v. 8). They were recompensing evil for evil (cf. Rom. 12:17). It is this basic moral fault, rather than the matter of improper or incorrect procedure, which Paul condemns. He is not advocating the setting up of Christian courts in order to do the thing right. He is advocating that they not do it at all.

D. *The Basic Misconception Behind It* (vv. 9-10)

Again the words, "Don't you know?" (v. 9), reveal their lack of understanding, their unclear thinking, regarding the moral requirements for participation in the kingdom of God. Paul proceeds now to state this basic principle in unmistakable terms. "The unrighteous shall not inherit the kingdom of God" (v. 9).[3]

There follows a specific list of sinners who are shut out of the kingdom (vv. 9-10). The list is the same as in 5:10-11 with four additions: (1) adulterers, a particular kind of fornicator, referring to infidelity within the married state; (2) effeminate, may refer to one who is soft or weak, a "sissy," but considering its location here it is far more probable that it is used in the technical sense of a man who submits to homosexual relations, a passive homosexual;[4] (3) abusers of themselves with mankind (KJV), or homosexuals (NASB). The vividly descriptive term which Paul uses in the original Greek ("one who goes to bed with a male") makes the meaning distinct; (4) thieves, those who steal by stealth, the sneak-thief, as compared with a robber who steals by force.

Thus these four additional terms add descriptive details to two of the general terms found in the earlier list. The first three further delineate the general category of sexual immorality ("fornication"). The last adds another to the category of "finan-

---

[3]The use of the article with "unrighteous" in the KJV and many other English versions has resulted in a peculiar misunderstanding of the thrust of this passage. "The unrighteous" suggests a specific class of people, and the description which follows identifies this class as "the unsaved." So the passage is understood to say that the unsaved shall not be saved, a rather meaningless tautology. There is no article in the Greek and its absence indicates he is not speaking of a class or a specific group but rather a characterization, a particular type of people, those who can be described by using the word "unrighteous people." "Don't fool yourself, those who live immoral lives . . . will have no share in His kingdom" (Kenneth N. Taylor, *Living Letters,* Tyndale House, Wheaton, 1962).

[4]Greek, *malakos.* See Arndt and Gingrich, *Lexicon.*

cial immorality," the covetous and extortioner·of the previous
list.

E. *The Utter Incongruity of It* (v. 11)

That such gross sins as listed in this catalog should exist among
Christians is an utterly unthinkable concept. Such indeed some
of them had been before they were saved, but that very statement implies that now it should be different. The word "but,"
three times repeated here, is a very strong adversative. Certainly they cannot be such now. Three things have happened to
change this situation. "You were washed[5] . . . sanctified . . .
justified." The aorist tense used in these three words probably
refers back to the historic moment at which they had become
Christians, or to the experiences by which they had become
separated from their old life. The order is given from the van-
tage point of their present Christian life, looking back on their
experience. The actual chronological order is in reverse.

F. *Summary of the Section*

This section and the preceding vividly express Paul's concept
of what it is to be a Christian, what the Christian life should be
like. His amazement, and the painful, almost angry, reaction
which bursts from his lips in these chapters reveal as clearly as
his expressed words the utter impropriety, even impossibility,
that such things can be true of a genuine brother in Christ. Such
immoralities as these surely are an evidence that a person is not
born again, that he is not ready for entrance into the kingdom of
God. Nor is this in any way in opposition to the basic Pauline
doctrine of salvation by grace through faith alone. He is not here
teaching a salvation by works. He is merely expressing what he
expresses many times elsewhere, what is expressed by many

---

[5]The form of the Greek word suggests "you washed yourselves," or
"you submitted yourselves for washing." The middle voice suggests
our part in the work of cleaning up our lives. Other occurrences of this
word are associated with baptism (cf. Acts 22:16) and the meaning
may be "you submitted yourselves for baptism." Therefore, these
things no longer have a place in your life; you are dead to them.

other writers of the New Testament,[6] that saving faith is always evidenced by a changed life, that a continuance in, or a return to, the old sinful ways is evidence that the profession of faith has never been genuine.

II. THE PROBLEM OF CHRISTIAN LIBERTY AND MORAL LAXITY (6:12-20)

The introduction of the subject of Christian liberty at this point suggests that the Corinthian Christians were defending their tolerance and broadmindedness toward the gross immoralities in their midst by appealing to that doctrine. The expression, twice repeated, "All things are lawful unto me" (v. 12) sounds very much as though it may have been one of the statements of the Corinthians themselves, quoted here by the Apostle Paul in order to answer it by putting it in its proper perspective.

A. *Christian Liberty and Its Counterbalances* (v. 12)

Paul takes up the Corinthians' claim and repeats it positively. It is true. Paul himself is the champion of Christian liberty. But the doctrine of Christian liberty must be safeguarded by two other principles. (1) The principle of expediency, "but all things are not expedient." The use of the word "expedient" here is unfortunate. Rather, it should be rendered "profitable," "useful," or "helpful." It refers to that which contributes or confers benefit upon someone. The exercise of Christian liberty is not always beneficial. (2) The principle of self-mastery. Here Paul uses a play on words. "All . . . are within my power. . . . I will not be brought under the power of any." Paul determines not to let his liberty make a slave out of him. After all, if he is *free* he doesn't *have* to exercise his freedom!

---

[6]The following list of similar passages is recommended for further study on this most important theme: Acts 8:13, 21-23; Rom. 6:1, 15; 8:5-9, 12, 13; I Cor. 5:7-8, 11; 6:9-20; II Cor. 6:14—7:1; 11:1-3; Gal. 5:19-21; Eph. 4:17-20; 5:5-8; Phil. 1:9-11; Col. 1:21-23; I Thess. 2:10-12; 4:1-7; Titus 2:11-12; Heb. 6:4-6; 10:26-31; James 2:14-26; 3:11-13; I Peter 3:8-12; II Peter 2:20-22; I John 1:5-6; 2:4, 9-11; 3:3, 4-10; 4:20; Rev. 21:8, 27; 22:15. Back of all these is the basic teaching of our Lord Jesus (e.g., Matt. 7:13-23).

B. *Christian Liberty and Its Proper Boundaries* (v. 13)

Paul, the great champion of Christian liberty, must often have said, "I am out from under the bondage of the law, I am free from all legal demands; all things are lawful to me." But, in this context he makes it clear that when he says "all things" he is not using that term in its broadest sense. There are some areas where Christian liberty applies; for example, in the matter of meats or food. "Food for the belly, the belly for food." These two correspond to each other. They suit each other. Both are temporary. God will put both of them out of use (Greek, *katargeō*). In the resurrection food and stomachs will not be needed. In other words, food and eating are matters which are morally indifferent, and a proper realm for Christian liberty to act.

But not so in the next example which Paul adduces. "The body is *not* for fornication." We may imply that some in Corinth were saying, "The body is for fornication, just like food is for the belly. Both are natural appetites and it is proper to seek satisfaction for both alike." Paul vehemently denies this analogy. This is an entirely different situation. The body belongs to the Lord. They correspond to each other; they suit each other. Notice how he calls the body a temple of God. It is His body (v. 15; cf. Eph. 5:30). The body is not temporary, but permanent (v. 14). It is going to be resurrected, transformed, and glorified, and we are going to keep it throughout eternity. Therefore, the use that we make of our bodies is not morally indifferent, and its abuse is outside the realm of Christian liberty. Christian liberty does not include fornication.

C. *The Sacredness of the Body* (vv. 15-20)

To support his contention that fornication is a sin against the body and therefore not subject to the principle of Christian liberty, Paul argues for the sacredness of the human body, and draws some implications from that fact (vv. 15-20).

1. *Our Bodies Are the Members of Christ* (vv. 15-17)

Even the reading of these verses shocks us. If our bodies are members of Christ's body, then for us to involve those bodies in fornication is equivalent to putting Christ in bed with a harlot, an utterly abhorrent idea. He goes on to point out that harlotry involves a kind of union (v. 16). But we are already joined in a spiritual union with Christ (v. 17). Fornication, therefore, is a kind of spiritual bigamy.

2. *Our Bodies Are Permanent* (v. 18)

Here is a rather difficult verse to interpret precisely, but its basic teaching is clear. Fornication is a sin against one's own body. It somehow permanently marks or shames our bodies. Therefore Paul says, "Flee fornication." To flee is the only proper way to handle this kind of temptation. Turn around and run. Don't try to fight it. Get away from it. Remember Joseph (Gen. 39:12).

3. *Our Bodies Are the Temple of the Holy Spirit* (vv. 19-20)

As temples, our bodies are not only the dwelling place of God, but also the peculiar property of God. Since they belong to God, they should be used to glorify God.

Questions for Discussion

1. Why is covetousness ranked with sins of immorality?

2. Is it always wrong for a Christian to be involved in court trials? Under what circumstances would it be permissible? Support your conclusions from Scripture.

3. Does Paul take literally the teaching of Christ on non-resistance and non-retaliation? In what way does his teaching differ from the Sermon on the Mount?

4. How can you reconcile the teaching of verse 9 with the scriptural teaching that salvation is by grace through faith alone?

5. Is there any scriptural basis for the present-day effort to make homosexuality respectable?

6. Is it ever wrong to do right? Is it ever right to do wrong? What is the difference?

Chapter 6

MARRIAGE COUNSELING

(7:1-40)

From the opening verse of this chapter it is clear that the apostle is answering a letter written to him by the Corinthian church. Perhaps they were replying to Paul's previous letter, asking for clearer instructions as to how they should live in relation to the fornicators of this world (cf. 5:9). Their letter evidently contained many questions, for apparently the rest of this epistle is devoted to answering these questions.[1] Unfortunately, we do not have their letter. We do not know precisely what their questions were. We have only the answers which Paul gave. It is a bit like listening to one side of a telephone conversation. We must surmise what the question was by studying the answer, then allow the understanding of the question to help in the interpretation of the answer.

I. ADVICE TO THE UNMARRIED (vv. 1-9)

Evidently the first question was, Is it good to get married? Should those who are unmarried remain single or get married? Perhaps there were some who were advocating celibacy as an extreme reaction to the prevalent immorality. Others were questioning the propriety of the single state.

A. *The Single State Is Good and Proper* (v. 1)

It is all right to remain single. The word "good" indicates it is right, honorable, morally proper (cf. our colloquial English, "okay"). "Not to touch a woman," means not to have sexual relationship with a woman, to be celibate, to remain unmarried.

Paul does not say that it is better to remain single. Paul is not disparaging marriage, but he is defending celibacy against those

---

[1]The clue to these questions is the recurring phrase "now concerning . . ." (Greek, *peri de*) found here in 7:1, also 7:25; 8:1; 12:1; 16:1.

who thought it wrong. He flatly says to be single is all right, it is proper, it is good.

B. *It May Be Better to Marry* (v. 2)

There was a particular situation involved at Corinth which prompted Paul to advise marriage, "to avoid fornication." This expression would better be translated, "in view of the immoralities." Corinth was a wicked city with all kinds of sexual immoralities prevalent. Under these circumstances, it might be better to marry.

Note Paul's insistence on "one's own" wife or husband (v. 2). To him, marriage involves absolute separation to one only. Only in such relationship is it good to touch a woman, i.e., one's own wife.

C. *If Married, Be Married* (vv. 3-5)

Paul makes it very clear that celibacy belongs to the unmarried, not to the married state. Evidently there was a feeling that sex was sinful, impure, even for the married. Paul, to the contrary, teaches that celibacy is sinful in the case of marriage. (1) Sex is a mutual obligation on the married (v. 3). The expression "render due benevolence" (KJV), "fulfill his duty" (NASB), "let him keep paying his debt" (literal translation), is a euphemistic expression for the obligation of carrying on the sexual responsibilities of the marriage relationship. (2) Married folks are not their own masters (v. 4). (3) To deny sex expression within marriage is a forceful robbery (v. 5; cf. same word in 6:7, 8). (4) Temporary exception may be made by mutual consent for spiritual reasons (v. 5), undelayed resumption of the relationship is mandatory (v. 5 lc).

D. *It Is a Matter of Individual Choice* (vv. 6-9)

Verse 6, along with verses 12 and 40, have frequently been used as an argument against the doctrine of inspiration, for Paul, supposedly, disclaims inspiration. Such, of course, is a complete misunderstanding of the passage. It might better be read, "by way of permission rather than by way of commandment." To marry, or not to marry, is not a matter of right and wrong, of duty, of commandment. Either state is permissible. God has given no command, "Thou shalt get married." To remain single is good (v. 1). To get married is good also (v. 38). Every man has his own gift (v. 7). Some have the gift of foregoing the blessings of married life for the sake of the kingdom of God (cf. Matt. 19:10-12). Others have the gift of being married and establishing a home, serving God in that way. The decision as to whether a person should get married or not should be made in the light of the gift which God has given him.

E. *Paul's Preference* (vv. 7a, 8)

There is no question that Paul's personal preference and advice favors the unmarried state, and he is loyal to his gift (cf. vv. 26, 32-33, 40). On the basis of such advice, some have accused the apostle of being a "woman hater," and opposed to marriage. It is an unfair and short-sighted accusation, as may be seen when we look at other teaching of the apostle on this subject (cf. I Tim. 5:14; Eph. 5:22-33).

Again Paul qualifies his recommendation of celibacy in view of the Corinthian situation. It is better to marry than to risk fornication (v. 9). The words "if they cannot contain" (Greek, "hold themselves in," "keep mastery over themselves") mean, "if they cannot control their sex craving and keep it under control." The solution then is, Let them marry. This is the God-given and holy provision for satisfaction of the sex passion. Within marriage, it is holy, proper, and good. It is better to marry and to have a proper and pure outlet for this passion than to remain unmarried and subject themselves to the dangerous temptation caused by unsatisfied passion. It is better, not in the sense that one is good and the other is bad. Both may be good. "It is better to marry than to burn, but if marriage is not possible, it is better infinitely to burn than to *sin*."[2]

Severe criticism has been addressed to Paul's discussion of marriage here because it is based wholly on the issue of sex. Certainly there are other and higher motivations and considerations in the matter of holy matrimony than this. Paul himself is aware of these and speaks of them on other occasions. Perhaps a

---

[2]Findlay, *Expositor's Greek*, p. 825.

few considerations will help us to understand the emphasis in this passage. (1) Remember, we have only the answers, not the questions. They may have asked the questions in such a way that Paul's answer dealt primarily with the sex problems involved. (2) Corinth was a place where sex was prominent, much like it is in our own day. Most of the problems of marriage were, and are, aggravated by the over-emphasis on sex. (3) Sex *is* a large element in marriage, and rightly so, for God so intended it. To emphasize the importance and holiness of sex in its relation to marriage, is not to belittle marriage, rather it is to put it on its proper scriptural foundation.

II. ADVICE TO THE MARRIED (vv. 10-24)

As his response to the unmarried was an answer to a written question from the Corinthian church, so we may assume that his next section dealing with advice to the married (see v. 10) is also in response to a specific question from them.

A. *The General Commandment of the Lord* (vv. 10-11)

Verse 10 makes it clear that in this case Paul is not dealing with a mere matter of permission. This is a commandment. It is *his* command as an inspired apostle. But more than that, it is a specific command given by the Lord Jesus Christ himself. It is the teaching of Jesus as found in the gospels, given while He was here in the flesh (see Matt. 5:32; 19:9; Mark 10:2-12; Luke 16:18). This command of our Lord categorically forbids all divorce.[3] It applies alike to husband and wife. In case the divorce has already occurred, it specifically forbids remarriage: "Let her remain unmarried." The only exception (actually, it is not an exception) is reconciliation[4] with the former husband.

---

[3]No mention is made here of the supposed exception found in the Matthew passages. Either he considered this as well known and understood, not calling for mention, or, he did not consider it as an exception. It is very improbable that he did not know of it.

[4]There is no conflict here with Deuteronomy 24:4. There, the forbidding of remarriage to the former husband was after she had been married to a second husband.

B. *A Particular Command of the Apostle* (vv. 12-16)

Paul has appealed to the clear, direct command of the Lord Jesus that marriage is the inviolable union of one man and one woman for life as the background for his answer to the particular problem raised by the Corinthians. The Lord's general statement had not said anything specific on this next point. So Paul speaks by the authority of inspiration to apply the principle taught by our Lord to the particular problem. What he says is no less binding (cf. v. 17 lc).

Their particular question had to do with mixed marriages, a case where a Christian is married to an unbeliever. How this situation arose is not stated. Most likely, it came about when one was converted after marriage. Possibly some Christians had married unbelievers in disobedience to the Lord's command (cf. v. 39). One way or another, there must have been many Christians in Corinth whose marriage partners were unbelievers. What should they do? The apostolic answer is clear and forthright. If the unbeliever is willing, let them remain married (vv. 12-14). Such a marriage is valid and holy. Some in Corinth may have thought otherwise, hence this question was raised. Marriage is a divine institution for the whole human race, not just for Christians. The marriage relationship is sanctified even in such mixed marriages. Otherwise their children would be illegitimate and that is unthinkable[5] (v. 14).

If, however, the unbelieving partner wants to separate, let him go (vv. 15-16). The believer is free from the obligation to preserve the marriage. Probably there is little he can do anyway for the unbeliever would hardly share his scruples against divorce. This word of the apostle would free the believer from any self-imposed stigma or blame for the separation which he could do nothing about. But the initiative for separation must come from the unbeliever, never from the believer.

---

[5]There are, of course, other interpretations of this passage, and the problem is complicated by the intrusion of the subject of infant baptism. For a fuller statement of the matter and an exposition of the view here presented, see Albert Barnes, Notes on the New Testament, *I Corinthians*, Baker Book House, Grand Rapids, 1962, pp. 115-116, and A. T. Robertson, *Word Pictures in the New Testament*, Harper, New York, 1931, p. 128.

Does that leave the believer free to marry? The answer must be an absolute, no. The general command of the Lord Jesus in the immediate context (vv. 10-11) forbids it, as does the whole teaching of Scripture on the subject. Marriage is a one man, one woman affair; the two become one, and it is for life (cf. v. 39) Rom. 7:2, 3). Anything else is fornication, adultery, bigamy, sin.

C. *The Principle Involved* (vv. 17-24 and v. 15 lc).

The principle which Paul uses to support his advice is stated, illustrated, and applied in the paragraph which follows. It may be variously described as the principle of peace, or the principle of contentment, or the principle of the status quo. In essence, what he is saying is, "Be satisfied with your state." If the unbelieving partner is willing to remain, don't you try to fight it. "God has called us to peace." Two illustrations are given. (1) Circumcision. Were you circumcised when you were saved? Then don't become uncircumcised. Were you uncircumcised when you were saved? Then don't become circumcised (vv. 18-19). (2) Slavery (vv. 21-23). Were you called as a slave? Don't worry about it; remember, you are the Lord's freeman. Of course, if you have a chance to get your liberty use it.

"God hath called us to peace" (v. 15). A Christian should be satisfied, not agitating for a change of state. This applies to remaining married or to letting them go. Verse 16 gives a reason for this attitude: Who knows if you will be able to save your husband (or wife)? Two opposite interpretations are possible. It may be taken as an argument against the believer accepting separation or divorce, based on the hope of saving their partner. Or, it may be taken as an argument in favor of accepting a separation. How do you know you will be able to save them by staying? While the second interpretation fits the context well, it seems so out of character from what we would expect the apostle to say that the present writer prefers the first interpretation.

III. ADVICE REGARDING VIRGINS (vv. 25-38)

A. *The Authority of This Advice* (v. 25)

Again, we may suppose that in this section Paul is answering a specific question addressed to him from the Corinthians. And, again, he explains the basis of his words. With regard to this matter, he has no direct statement of Jesus. Neither has he a command by inspiration (cf. v. 6). This is another case of "permission"; either course of action is right or good. As he did in the case of his advice to the unmarried (vv. 1-9), so here Paul will recommend one course of action: "It is my considered judgment[6] that this is good" (v. 26). And although this is advice, not a commandment, yet it is good advice, worthy of serious consideration inasmuch as it comes from the Apostle Paul who was graciously considered of God to be faithful (cf. a similar expression in v. 40).

B. *Two Interpretations*

The section before us is a difficult one and has given rise to two widely different interpretations:

(1) That it refers to a father giving his virgin daughter in marriage, or refraining from doing so.[7]

(2) That it refers to a man preserving his own "virginity" by refraining from marrying his girl friend.[8] For several reasons, the present writer prefers the first of these interpretations. (a) The other view would seem to be a mere repetition of verses 1 to 9, advice not to get married. (b) The idea of a perpetual engagement, or a partner-in-celibacy, introduces a very strange and unwholesome situation wholly out of harmony with the Biblical view of marriage. (c) The first view is in accord with the marriage customs of the ancient world. In those days there was no individual courting. Marriages were arranged by parents.

---

[6]Greek, *nomizō*. The KJV, "I suppose," is too weak.

[7]This is the interpretation reflected in the KJV and the NASB. *The Jerusalem Bible* (Doubleday, Garden City, New York, 1966) gives a very clear translation according to this interpretation. For a full consideration of the passage from the viewpoint of this interpretation see Lenski, *Corinthians,* pp. 325-331.

[8]This view understands the word "virgin" (vv. 25, 36, 37) to mean his "betrothed" (Weymouth [*New Testament in Modern Speech,* Harper, New York], RSV [*Revised Standard Version,* Nelson, New York, 1952]); or "partner in celibacy" (NEB); or, "a spiritual bride" (Moffatt [New Translation, Hodder and Stoughton, London, 1953]). TEV renders it "an engaged couple who have decided not to marry."

Thus a very natural situation arose. Christian parents in Corinth were asking Paul's advice as to whether or not they should arrange a marriage for their marriageable children. (d) The word used in verse 38 (Greek, *gamizō*) strictly means "to give in marriage" (cf. Matt. 24:38). This meaning demands the first interpretation and forbids the second.

C. *The Advice* (vv. 26, 27, 32, 35)

Under the circumstances Paul advises that it is better to be unmarried. He mentions three things about these circumstances which make this preferable. (1) "The present distress" (vv. 26-28). It was a time of persecution and trouble. Marriage would aggravate the situation. (2) "The time is short" (vv. 29-31). This shortness of time is variously interpreted as (a) until the coming of the Lord, (b) until the storm of persecution breaks on them, (c) a general expression meaning the transitoriness of the present order. The first of these seems most natural, except that it would make the advice of Paul against marriage an advice which would be valid in every age including our own, a notion which hardly can be correct. The third is a general statement which obviously is true, but the same objection applies to it as to the first. Perhaps the second interpretation, then, is preferable. (3) "I would have you without carefulness" (vv. 32-35). Paul would spare them from the anxieties which accompany the responsibility of marriage and home, coveting for them the freedom to devote themselves wholly to the service of the Lord. It is worthy to note that the apostle recognized the responsibilities of family as valid claims upon the attention of the believer, even taking precedence over service for Christ (cf. I Tim. 5:8).

IV. ADVICE TO WIDOWS (vv. 39, 40)

Should a widow remarry? Paul explains that death, and only death, breaks a marriage relationship. Hence the survivor is free to marry. Of course, the general requirement still applies, "only in the Lord." However, Paul's judgment is again, "She is happier" if she remains unmarried. This is said in view of the same adverse circumstances which he has already put forth earlier in the chapter. Under other circumstances he gives exactly the opposite advice (I Tim. 5:11, 14). We may assume therefore that the same principle would apply to the other advices given in this chapter. For example, it may be possible, even probable, that ministers and missionaries, under our present circumstances, might better be married.

The teaching of this chapter may be summarized under two propositions. (1) If you are unmarried you are free to choose according to your own gift. Take into consideration all the circumstances and act accordingly. (2) If you are married remain so, and be faithful to your marriage responsibilities.

Questions for Discussion

1. Is it proper for Christians to tell old maid and bachelor jokes? Or to make fun of and ridicule the single person?

2. Are there those who have been prompted into an unwise marriage by undue pressure from folks who felt that somehow it wasn't right to remain single?

3. Was Paul getting out of his proper place when he taught the mutual obligation of sex in marriage? Is this lesson needed today? Should God's ministers preach it?

4. Does Paul's advice reflect an unwholesome attitude toward women, sex, and marriage?

5. Should a Christian neglect his family to serve the Lord?

6. Is the hope of Christ's early return a reason for not marrying?

Chapter 7

FREE: TO DO WHAT?

(8:1–10:33)

Meats offered to idols were the specific occasion of their next question, but the real problem involved in this section is Christian liberty. Paul has already raised this issue in 6:12-18. Now he turns to a fuller discussion of it.

I. MEATS OFFERED TO IDOLS (Chap. 8)

A. *What Was This Problem?*

A mere reading of the section, particularly 8:1, 4, 7, 10 and 10:25, 27, shows that the problem had to do with a difference of opinion and practice among Christians regarding the use of meat which had been offered as sacrifices to idols. Such offering was a common practice in pagan Corinthian society. The Christian could be confronted with this problem in at least three ways. (1) Eating in heathen temples. Public affairs, even social gatherings, frequently were held in the idol temple. Probably this was often the only available place and would be used as a "social hall" by the entire community even when the nature of the meeting would not be at all religious or related to the idol. Christians might attend banquets held in such a hall, and the meat would probably have been offered before the idol. (2) Buying meat in the meat market[1] (cf. 10:25). Even meat which was intended to be sold in the market was often consecrated by a token offering to the idol. Hence, when a Christian bought meat at the market there was always the possibility that it had

---

[1]Greek, *makellon*: A late Greek word borrowed from the Latin, referring to the shops where meat was sold. The "shambles" of the KJV is meaningless to most today. In the area of the shops opening on the Agora archeologists have discovered a fragmentary inscription containing the Latin form of the word (Jack Finegan, *Light from the Ancient Past*, Princeton University Press, Princeton, 1959, p. 361).

Temple of Apollo. Only remains of Greek Corinth. Levant Photo Service.

been so offered. (3) Invited to dinner by friends (cf. 10:27). It must often have happened that Christians were invited by unsaved friends and neighbors to eat with them, with no guarantee, of course, of the source of the meat served. It is to be presumed that this problem would not arise when they were invited by believers. Among the Christians at Corinth arose two different viewpoints as to how Christians should respond to this situation. Some considered such food defiled. They not only refused to eat themselves, but were offended by those who did eat. Others considered meat in the category of "morally indifferent things" and claimed Christian liberty. They considered it right to do so and went ahead.

It has become customary among modern Christians to designate these two groups as the "weak" and the "strong." The Bible does use these words in this connection, but not at all in the strong divisive sense in which it is frequently used today. Twice in this passage, Paul uses the word "weak," and twice more he makes it clear that their weakness was in the realm of the conscience. In the parallel passage, Romans 14 and 15, they are spoken of as weak in respect to faith. Nowhere in this Corinthian passage does he use the word "strong," and only once in the parallel passage (Rom. 15:1). Completely absent from both passages is the sense of arrogant superiority and belittling condescension which the terms so often connote as they are used today.[2]

B. *The Two Principles Involved* (vv. 1-3)

Two words are thrust prominently forward at the opening of this discussion, each representing a principle affecting this problem. Paul puts them in marked contrast in verse 1, "knowledge

---

[2] The word "weak" (Greek, *asthenēs*) was often used in the literal sense of physical weakness or illness and is involved in many of Christ's miracles of healing. It is frequently translated "infirmities." Its essential meaning is "helpless"; or even better, "those who need help." The word "strong" (Greek, *dynatoi*) is its opposite. It indicates one who is able, capable, sufficient for the task. To get a proper perspective on these words one should study carefully II Cor. 11:29 and 12:9, 10.

puffs up; love builds up."[3] Paul is probably making reference to some of their own claims, even quoting their very words, when he says, "We know that we all have knowledge." He does so a bit sarcastically, for in verse 7 he says that they did *not* all have this knowledge.

C. *The Principle of Knowledge Teaches Freedom* (vv. 4-6)

Applying now these principles to the problem at hand, our knowledge tells us that "an idol is nothing" (v. 4). Since there is only one God, then an idol is a false god, a fake, no god at all; it is nothing. Of course, there are many so-called gods, but Christians who have knowledge know that "there is but one God, the Father . . . and one Lord Jesus Christ" (v. 6). Applying this knowledge[4] to the present problem, if idols are nothing then they cannot hurt meat. Holding meat in front of a piece of wood or stone doesn't change the nutritional value of the meat one bit, nor does it impart any defilement to the meat. Therefore it is all right to eat meat that has been offered to idols.

D. *The Principle of Love Teaches Considerateness* (vv. 7-13)

The principle of knowledge says, "Go ahead and eat"; but, the principle of love says, "How will it affect others?" Verse 7 does not use the word love. But in it Paul raises the question of how others will feel about it, how it will affect others, and that is the very heart of love.

1. *Some Do Not Know This*

Some, probably many, in the Corinthian church did not have this clear-cut knowledge of the non-existence and unreality of idols. They had been converted from paganism. The idol had been a very real thing to them before, and even now it represents to them a very real memory of their old life and the things

---

[3]The play on words is in English only, but the original shows a similarly vivid play in sense.

[4]While this knowledge is factually correct and the conclusion Paul draws from it here is theoretically true, yet it is not the end of the story. Before concluding that this was Paul's own judgment of the matter, read 10:19, 20.

they had put behind them. When they ate meat which had been offered to idols, they did so with a very real conscience or consciousness of that fact. It reminded them vividly of their former practices, and in revulsion they said, "We ought not to be doing this."

2. Practicing Freedom Is Not a Virtue; Refraining from Freedom Does Not Harm (v. 8)

There is a strange perversion of thought about freedom, even of Christian liberty: If we are free to do a thing we feel that we *must* do it. We become slaves to our own freedom (cf. 6:12c). Paul reminds the Corinthians that exercising our freedom to eat meat does not approve us to God, nor does it make us any better. And the failure to exercise our freedom to eat does not hurt us any. So why not exercise our Christian liberty *not* to eat meat that is offered to idols?

3. Your Liberty Might Destroy a Brother (vv. 9-12)

Three times these weak ones are called "brothers." The term can only mean that they are Christian believers, or at least professing Christians.

The temptation to which these weak brethren are being subjected is expressed in verse 10. When they see the one who had knowledge (i.e., the knowledge that an idol is nothing, vv. 4-6) eating in the idol temple they may be tempted to say, "There is Mr. So-and-So. He is a strong Christian and he is eating meat offered to idols; perhaps my scruples are unwarranted. I will go ahead and eat too." Thus, although his conscience still condemns him, he is "emboldened"[5] to participate in an action which to him is sin. Thus, the liberty of the strong becomes an enticement to the weak to sin.

---

[5]The Greek word *oikodomeō* means literally, "to build up," "to edify" (v. 1). In every other occurrence in the New Testament it is used in a good sense. Only here is it used as an edification towards evil. Perhaps Paul is sarcastically throwing back at the strong their own words of reproach. They may have been saying, "The trouble with you is that you need to be built up." They were being "built up" all right — "strengthened" (NASB), emboldened to sin.

The danger to the weak brother is threefold. (1) Their "conscience is defiled" (cf. v. 7), they feel guilty. (2) They are caused to stumble (v. 9), enticed to sin. The liberty of those who feel free to eat may become a dangerous obstacle in their path, causing them to trip up and to fall. (3) The weak brother may "perish" (v. 11). This word (Greek, *apollumi*) is a very strong one. When used of persons it indicates ruin, destruction, death, and especially the eternal lostness of the unregenerate soul in hell (e.g., John 3:16). So far as this writer has been able to discover it is never used of a temporary hurt, or damage in this life.

How does this passage relate to the doctrine of eternal security? The present writer believes that the Scriptures teach that one who has received God's work of saving grace along with all its attendent miracles is eternally secure and shall ultimately come into glory. He does *not* accept the unscriptural caricature of that doctrine which makes it a license for sin, or uses it to minimize the awfulness of sin. Since the Scriptures do not contradict themselves, there must be a way to explain this verse. (1) Some would make the word "perish" refer to some temporary harm in this life, but what other damage could there possibly be to warrant the use of the word "perish"? Surely Paul is not saying that the weak brother who is emboldened to eat meat offered to idols will be visited with physical death for his crime! (2) I prefer to find the explanation in another direction. Paul is writing to a congregation, presumably made up of Christian believers. In such a group there always may be those who are mere professors, who call themselves Christians, who are known to the rest as Christian brothers, but who have never really experienced genuine salvation. Such perhaps were some of these "weak brothers." These, by being emboldened to sin against their conscience, are turned aside from that genuine surrender to Christ, and thus perish eternally. (3) Whatever explanation may be offered, the warnings in the Bible are to be taken seriously.

But there is also a danger to the strong (v. 12). The one who insists on his right to exercise his freedom involves himself in a twofold sin. (1) He sins against his brothers, wounding their weak conscience. The word translated "wounding" means literally "to beat," "to smite." Thus their unwholesome influence keeps pounding, hammering away at the weak spot of their weak brethren until they break. (2) He sins against Christ, robbing Him of the results of His death. The seriousness of these sins is brought out vividly in the last clause of verse 11, "for whom Christ died." Note the terrible contrast. Christ *died* for him; *you* will not even give up a meal for him! Christ gave His life for him. You will not give up your precious right to exercise Christian liberty. This sentence forms a climax to the whole passage.

4. *Paul's Rule* (v. 13)

Paul closes this chapter by expressing his own principle of conduct in such matters. He is determined to safeguard the exercise of Christian liberty by a self-denying concern for the wellbeing of others. "If meat make my brother to offend, I will eat no flesh." Surely this is a small sacrifice to make when the risks are so great. In understanding this statement, it is important to interpret correctly the word "offend" (Greek, *skandalizō*). The figure back of this word is that of a "trigger" of a trap; hence, "that which causes one to be entrapped," and then, "an enticement to sin," "to cause to sin." Paul is not giving up meat merely to avoid hurting their feelings or displeasing them. He says, in effect, "If my eating meat will entice a brother to commit sin, I will eat no meat."

II. PAUL'S EXAMPLE (Chap. 9)

A. *What Liberty Permitted* (vv. 1-14)

The principle of Christian liberty is still under consideration in this chapter. Paul uses his own example in other areas of his life in order to illustrate the principle he has been advocating in the preceding chapter, and at the same time to broaden the base upon which that principle is built. He begins with a series of rhetorical questions asserting his authority and listing some of the rights which he was free to exercise as an apostle.[6] This authority involved his right (1) to eat and drink (v. 4); (2) to

---

[6]Already there are indications that there were enemies of Paul in Corinth who were questioning his apostleship. This will occupy a major portion of Paul's second letter to the Corinthians.

have a wife (v. 5); (3) to expect the support of the churches so that it would be unnecessary for him to work for his support (v. 6).

Particularly with regard to this last, Paul expands his illustration. He defends his right to financial support by appealing to a series of arguments. (1) Argument from human analogy (v. 7). Three parallel examples show that such is the rule in all of life. The soldier, the farmer, and the shepherd all participate in the rewards of their own labor. (2) Argument from Scripture (vv. 8-10). He quotes Deuteronomy 25:4 and sees in it not so much God's concern for the well-being of the ox, but even more his concern that the person who serves the Lord in the harvest field should do so in hope of participating in the physical results of the harvest. (3) Argument from the common sense of what is right (vv. 11-12). (4) Argument from actual practice (v. 13). As a matter of fact, those who ministered in holy things in the temple did get their support from the temple. This would be true in both the Jewish and the pagan world. (5) Argument from the word of Jesus (v. 14). Probably this is a reference to our Lord's saying, "The laborer is worthy of his hire" (Luke 10: 7; Matt. 10:10).

B. *The Principle of Self-Denial* (vv. 12b, 15-27)

Although Paul argues so convincingly of the rightness of the laborer expecting financial support for his spiritual service, yet he himself did not claim that right. He could have done so with all propriety. He certainly did not question either the right or the propriety of others using this privilege. But he himself was prompted by a higher principle, a consideration for the well-being of the Corinthians, which prompted him to forego his privilege. He gives us three reasons for his action.

1. *For the Sake of the Gospel* (vv. 15-18, 23)

Paul has in mind a higher reward than the benefit of material support. Indeed, his sense of responsibility toward the gospel was too strong to allow thinking of it as a way of making a living. Pay for preaching the gospel? Never! That was a stewardship laid on him. To do it earned no credit, deserved no pay.

He was but a slave doing his duty (cf. Luke 17:7-10). But there was one thing Paul could do to please his Master and gain a basis for pride in his work. He could voluntarily renounce his right to support, support himself, and make the gospel without cost to those he served! "If I were volunteering my services of my own free will, then the Lord would give me a special reward; but that is not the situation, for God has picked me out and given me this sacred trust and I have no choice. Under this circumstance, what is my pay? It is the special joy I get from preaching the Good News without expense to anyone, never demanding my rights."[7]

2. *For the Sake of Souls* (vv. 19-22)

These verses bring us to the very heart of the motivating force which drove Paul to this and every other act of self-denial, his love for lost souls. Though he was free, yet he deliberately made himself a slave to all that he might win the more — "all things to all men, that I might by all means save some." To win the Jews, he was willing to forego his liberty and subject himself to the burdens of the law. To win the Gentiles who were without law, he was willing to forego his personal preference for the higher Jewish standards.[8] To those weak ones who were having trouble with the meats offered to idols, Paul was willing to put himself in their place in order that he might win them. All this he is willing to do for the sake of the gospel in order that he might, along with them, share in its blessings (v. 23).

3. *For the Sake of Self* (vv. 24-27)

Still another motive prompted Paul's refusal to exercise his Christian liberty and that was his determination to experience self-mastery. Paul knew the propensity of the human heart toward selfishness, laziness, fleshliness. He constantly fought it, even when it was not wrong or sinful in itself, because he was

---

[7]Taylor, *Living Letters.*

[8]Note the parenthesis (v. 21). Even Paul, the champion of Christian liberty, could not quite bear to let that statement stand in its raw nakedness. Without law? Well, not quite! Not without God's law; but under Christ's law.

determined to remain his own master. He draws illustrations from the sports world of his day, the runner and the boxer, and their willingness to endure the rigors of training and self-discipline for the sake of an uncertain and a corruptible crown. So he kept buffeting his body and making it his slave, "lest possibly, after I have preached to others, I myself should be disqualified"[9] (NASB).

III. A SCRIPTURAL EXAMPLE (10:1-15)

A. *The Israelites in the Wilderness* (vv. 1-5)

Next Paul turns to the Old Testament Scriptures[10] for another illustration. He recites the story of the exodus of the children of Israel from Egypt, emphasizing the high spiritual privileges which they all had in common, then reminds them that in spite of these blessings many did not please God.

B. *The Application to the Corinthians* (vv. 6-12)

Direct and specific application of this Old Testament story is brought home to the Corinthians. Paul begins and ends this section with a general rule of application (vv. 6, 11). The idea back of the word "example" (Greek, *typos*) is "a pattern," "a mold," a "type" of experience which we can use to fashion our own lives. In fact, these "typical" characteristic experiences of the Israelites were written down for the express purpose of putting *us* in mind of the same truths, for we who live in the gospel

---

[9]Greek, *adokimos*; literally, "not approved," "tested and found wanting." In the context of athletic games it meant "disqualified" (e.g., for breaking the training rules; cf. II Tim. 2:5). The danger is losing his crown, his reward, not his salvation.

[10]If it surprises us that Paul would expect a Gentile church in Corinth to be familiar with the Jewish Old Testament Scriptures, it should remind us of the central place which the Scriptures occupied in the apostolic program of evangelism. Paul himself had preached 18 months in Corinth. His successor, Apollos, was "mighty in the scriptures" (Acts 18:24) and it is not unlikely that the church there had regular Bible study classes. Paul did not want them to be ignorant of the Scriptures (cf. v. 1).

age are the proper recipients of the lessons of all ages (v. 11, NASB).

In between these general applications are listed a series of specific warnings (vv. 6-10).

C. *A Final Sobering Application* (vv. 12-14)

Here now is the whole point of this Old Testament illustration. They all started out with the same spiritual provision, but "with many of them God was not well pleased: for they were overthrown in the wilderness" (v. 5). What had happened? They had let down their guard. They had become victim to sins which were not expected from those with such high spiritual privilege. Paul's conclusion is, "Let him that thinketh he standeth take heed lest he fall" (v. 12).

Arguments about Christian freedom, the right to do some questionable thing, are seldom a mere matter of freedom. There is frequently a real danger of falling. Such has been in the mind of Paul ever since he began his discussion of the subject of eating meats offered to idols, and these "strong" Christians who felt so sure that they knew the nothingness of idols, were actually skating on thin ice. Paul warns them: Beware. Look at what happened to the Israelites. Flee from idolatry (v. 14). Idolatry is a sin like adultery. The only safe course is to "flee." Don't play around with it. Stay away from it as far as you can.

Verse 13 is put in as a gracious encouragement to both strong and weak in the face of this ever-present danger. It is an unqualified promise from God, based upon His own faithfulness, that *you need not fall.* He knows how strong, and how weak, you are, and He promises never to allow any temptation to come against you which is too hard for you. He promises that with every temptation He does permit to come He sends along with it the necessary "way out" of it. If Christians once learn the meaning of I Corinthians 10:13 they never again will say, "I couldn't help it."

IV. THE LESSON FROM THE COMMUNION SERVICE (vv. 16-22)

Still in the context of eating meat offered to idols, Paul appeals to them as sensible, reasonable men to draw their own conclusions (v. 15). The communion of the bread and the cup, instituted by our Lord on the eve of His sacrificial death, was a familiar practice to them. They understood well that the partaking of the communion elements was a communing with, a partaking of, Christ. So also it was in Israel. Those who ate of the sacrifices were partakers of the altar. So also, Paul reasons, is it in paganism. Those who partook of the idol sacrifices were communing with the idols. Not that the stone or wood image was anything, but it represented a false religious system which was in actuality the worship of demons (vv. 19, 20). Such a mixing of the table of the Lord with the table of demons was a monstrous thought and a moral impossibility. God is a jealous God, and to provoke His jealousy by playing around with idolatry is the utmost in foolishness; unless, of course, you are greater than He is! (v. 22).

V. THE FINAL SUMMARY OF THE PROBLEM (vv. 23-33)

A. *A Repetition of the Principle* (vv. 23-24)

Paul now draws to a conclusion his treatment of this problem of Christian liberty[11] and its relationship to the specific problem of eating meats offered to idols. (1) He repeats the basic principle expressed in Chapter 8, the principle of concern for the profit and well-being of others. (2) He reasserts the truth of Christian liberty (vv. 25-27). Paul has not abandoned his concept of Christian liberty. He still understands that meat offered

---

[11]F. W. Grosheide, in his *Commentary on the First Epistle to the Corinthians* (*New International Commentary* series), Eerdmans, Grand Rapids, 1968, p. 188, expressed clearly this balance in Paul's treatment of Christian liberty: "Here again there were two opinions concerning the matter and both were wrong. Some thought that the Christian was allowed to do all things; others did not understand the doctrine of Christian liberty correctly. The church had consulted Paul concerning this matter in her letter to him and had apparently asked him for a precise statement as to how to act. But the apostle does not make such a statement. Starting from the right principle he turns against both opinions, condemning one as an undue inclusivism and the other as an undue narrowness." (Cf. also the refreshingly clear insight of Ned B. Stonehouse in his foreword to Grosheide's book, p. 6.)

to idols is perfectly good meat, that it is not wrong in itself to eat it. He advises them to avoid over-scrupulousness. If you buy meat in the meat market or if you are invited out to dinner where meat is served, do not ask questions for conscience sake. Do not raise the issue of whether or not it has been offered to idols. That fact, in itself, is not important. In other words, practice your liberty wherever it does not offend or entice to sin. Of course, if someone raises the question, it is obvious that his conscience is having a problem, and out of considerateness and love for him you should forego the exercise of your liberty. (3) He reemphasizes his rule of respect for the other person (vv. 28-33).

Perhaps some general observations on this whole principle will be in order in concluding this chapter. In what situations should we be expected to forego our rights in deference to the uninstructed consciences of the weak brother? The scriptural context specifically applies it to (1) eating meat offered to idols (I Cor. 8-10 and Rom. 14), (2) eating unclean foods (Rom. 14), (3) the observance of special days (Rom. 14), (4) the right to be married (I Cor. 9), (5) the right of a minister to financial support (I Cor. 9), (6) the Jew-Gentile distinction (I Cor. 9: 20-22). It is to be noted that all of these are "morally indifferent" according to scriptural standards. None of them are matters which are right or wrong of themselves. Therefore, Scripture uses this principle of considerateness for the weaker brother as a *secondary* principle. It is to be used *only* if the issue of right or wrong is not involved. If the Bible says a thing is wrong, then this principle has no application whatever. The way it is frequently used by Christians to answer the questions of "worldly amusements" can hardly be justified unless it has first been determined that the particular worldly amusement under consideration is by scriptural standards not wrong in itself. It is interesting to note that in such applications, the "weak" are usually the stricter, whereas the "strong" are more broad. Apparently it is the mature, developed, "strong" conscience which is *less* sensitive to these worldly things. Unless one can conceive of increasing "worldliness" as an indication of greater spritituality, it becomes obvious that the whole application of this principle is a mistake in such cases.

Questions for Discussion

1. Why does liberty tend to become license? Does it work that way in social and political affairs? Is this what is back of our violent demonstrations and our permissive society?

2. Are the most spiritual people you know characterized by an attitude of permissiveness?

3. Have you known anyone who was lost to Christ and the church because of the influence of Christians practicing liberty?

4. Should churches pay their pastors a good salary? Should preachers make salary a major factor in their consideration of a call?

5. Do Christians today practice idolatry? commit fornication? tempt the Lord? murmur or complain? What is the result?

6. To what specific problems which we face as Christians can Paul's teaching of this principle be properly applied?

Chapter 8

PROPRIETY IN PUBLIC WORSHIP

(11:1-34)

A new subject is under discussion as we come to Chapter 11. There is no reference here to a written question from the Corinthians such as marked the beginning of the last two sections, but it may reasonably be implied from the wording of verse 2. It sounds very much like a reference to some background information which they may have furnished Paul as an introduction to their question. Actually, two topics are dealt with in this chapter, both of them having to do with matters of propriety in public worship.

I. WOMEN'S PROPER HEADCOVERING (vv. 2-16)

A. *Some Background Material*

The nature of this subject demands that we begin with some background considerations. The fact that the practice here referred to is only rarely observed today and its spiritual significance even more rarely understood, together with the revolution currently taking place regarding women's role in society, makes this subject a difficult one to deal with. At the same time it makes it a relevant and important one.

1. *Public Worship Is under Consideration Here*

Several considerations combine to make it probable that the headcovering dealt with in this passage was to be worn in connection with public worship of the church, not a question of wearing it on the street or in the home. (1) The two matters dealt with in this chapter are treated as parallel matters. It is clear that the second deals with propriety in public worship, and by analogy the first probably does also. These were both matters which the Apostle Paul had "delivered over" (vv. 2, 23) to the church in oral instruction. (2) The wearing of the headcovering is specifically related to "praying or prophesying" (vv. 4, 5).

Acrocorinth. Ancient Corinth lay at its foot, right center of the picture. Photo by author.

These activities relate particularly to public worship (cf. 14:3-4, 14-16, 23, 24). (3) Women did prophesy in the early church. While the role of women in the early church is a matter of sharp disagreement, it seems clear from this passage and from Acts 21: 9 that the women in the early church did participate in the public service. Their prominent role is also seen in the frequent mention of individuals, e.g., Priscilla. This does not contradict I Corinthians 14:34 where the context makes it clear that Paul is forbidding the speaking in tongues rather than all speaking. Nor does it contradict I Timothy 2:12 which, if read without the first comma, may be understood to forbid women "to teach or to usurp authority *over the man*," rather than forbidding all teaching or speaking in a church.

2. *The Covering Was an Artificial Covering*

The word used (Greek, *katakaluptō*) means simply "to cover," "to conceal." It was used in the Greek Old Testament of a veil worn by a harlot (Gen. 38:15), of the covering of the tabernacle (Exod. 26:14), and of the wings which covered the face and feet of the cherubim (Isa. 6:2). In the second century, a Christian writer, Hermes,[1] used it of a veil which covered a woman "as far as the forehead." That it was not another term for the hair in this passage is clear from verse 6, where substituting the word "hair" for "covering" makes nonsense, and verse 15 where a different word is used in the Greek for a covering when it refers to the hair.

Concerning the nature of this covering, we know practically nothing, except that it was worn to cover the head. It apparently was not a veil which covered the face. Perhaps its closest modern counterpart would be the general term, "hat."

3. *Its Significance Is Clearly Stated*

It marked the woman's subordination to the headship of the man (vv. 3-5, 7). *How* it signified this we can no longer discern. There seems to be no natural relationship between the covering itself and the thing it signified, at least none that can be discerned today.

---

[1]Visions 4, 2, 1.

What other significance it may have had we cannot be sure. Some have thought that the covering was a mark of purity, of decency, of virtue. And perhaps this is reflected in verse 6, "if it be a shame. . . ." As a matter of fact, we do not know enough about the custom to be dogmatic. Were harlots shaved? Perhaps, as a badge of shame when caught, but certainly not in the ordinary pursuit of their trade. Did harlots go without the veil? Probably the very opposite was true (cf. Gen. 38:14, 15 where the woman was identified as a harlot by the fact that she was wearing a covering). All that is known certainly is what can be learned from this passage. The covering signified the submission of the woman to her husband. Anything more than that is mere guesswork.

4. *Modern Application*

The problem of this passage is not in understanding its meaning. Rather it is knowing what to do about it, what to do with it. Three attitudes have been manifested.

a. Most would simply dismiss it as an ancient social custom which no longer is relevant. And in the light of many modern trends this view is probably least controversial. But it hardly satisfies the one who seriously considers the Bible as God's Word. Paul relates this practice to nature, to creation, to angels, to the divinely ordained order of headship. These arguments are not changing customs; with one possible exception they are all permanently valid arguments, as true today as they were when Paul gave them. To say the custom is no longer relevant is to say that Paul's arguments are no longer relevant.

b. Some would apply it spiritually, rather than literally. They would make the principle back of it (i.e., "a spirit of subjection") binding and permanently valid, but not the immediate expression of that principle in this social custom. This view also comes far from satisfying the facts of the case. Certainly Paul, at the time he wrote, was primarily concerned about the "spirit of subjection" and its spiritual significance. But he still commands them to observe the social custom. This view leaves unanswered the question: Just how should the "spirit of subjection" express itself today?

c. Some accept it as a valid part of Scripture *to be practiced today.* These hold that a godly Christian woman today, when she is participating publicly in the activities of the church, should consciously and deliberately indicate her scriptural role of subordination to the man by wearing a covering on her head, perhaps a hat or a "prayer covering."[2] The objection immediately thrown against this view is that it is no longer meaningful, that the wearing of a hat in church no longer signifies subjection to the husband. This, of course, is true. But why is it true? The reason is the failure of the church to *teach* its significance. The same argument is used against the washing of the saints' feet, and against baptism, both of which are based on ancient customs which are totally without significance today apart from proper teaching. It seems far better to inaugurate the proper training than to repeal the divinely given ordinances.

B. *The Development of the Argument*

Paul supports his ordinance with a series of eight arguments.

1. The woman's place in the divine order teaches the necessity for a covering (vv. 1-5, 7). This divine order is the same as is presented consistently elsewhere in Scripture. Paul's argument is that their relative place in that divine order dictates that a man should worship with his head uncovered[3] while the woman should worship with her head covered. The man "has no (intervening) lord in creation (cf. 9); he stands forth in worship,

---

[2]The distinctive little white lace covering used by certain church groups for this purpose is an effective testimony to their desire to observe the apostle's teaching. But there is nothing in this passage which suggests that a special covering was meant. Paul's admonition was to wear the ordinary covering, rather than to go bareheaded.

[3]Paul's statement that a man who prays with his head covered dishonors his head (v. 4) probably implies that the present Jewish practice of men covering their heads in worship is a later development. There is nothing in the passage, nor any evidence elsewhere, that Paul was deliberately reversing his former Jewish custom and inaugurating a new Christian order. A Jewish rabbi explained to the present writer that the Jewish practice is based on the scriptural injunction that they should not be as the Gentiles; Gentiles prayed and showed respect by uncovering their heads, so they do the opposite.

amidst his family, with no visible superior, holding headship direct from his Maker, and brought by his manhood into direct responsibility to Him 'through whom are all things.' "[4] In contrast, the woman has an intermediate head, the man, and her recognition of that proper order is expressed by wearing a covering.

It should be understood clearly that the term "head" and its corresponding opposite, "subjection" (cf. Eph. 5:24) have to do with rank, position, authority; not at all with ability. They denote positions in the governmental or administrative organization of affairs. They do not in any way reflect inferiority or inequality. Proof of this is seen in the relationship attributed within the Godhead. Christ is every bit as much God as God the Father. He is equal in essence. But, He is second person in the Godhead and subordinate to the Father in function (cf. 15:28; John 4:34; 5:18, 19). In another realm, an army captain may not be a better man, either physically or intellectually or morally, than the private. But he is superior in rank and function. So the Christian wife, even though she may be superior to her husband in ability, in personality, even in spirituality, yet she recognizes his headship and "ranks herself under" him in the divine economy of the home.

2. Social propriety argues for a covering (vv. 5, 6). The point of the argument here turns on the shamefulness of an unnatural uncovering of the woman's head through being shorn, i.e., having her hair cut off or having her head shaved. To remove the artificial covering is the same kind of act as to remove the natural covering. They are both shameful. The present writer, before he came to his present convictions on this subject, used to use verse 6 as support for the notion that this is merely a social custom of the day which is no longer relevant. This verse says, "If it be a shame. . . ." Then he reasoned: But it is no longer a shame for a woman to have her hair cut, therefore it is no longer a shame for her to remove the covering. But please note that Paul is not speaking of a woman having her hair cut *short*; he is speaking of having it cut off or shaven, and that *still* is a shame, even in the social patterns of today.

---

[4]Findlay, *Expositor's Greek*, p. 871.

3. The scriptural account of creation argues for a covering (vv. 7-9). Here, Paul develops the same basic reasoning as in (1) above, this time relating it to the facts of creation as revealed in the Scripture. According to it the creation of man and of woman were not parallel. Man was created first, directly from God's hand. The woman was created later, taken from man's side. These facts argue further, in Paul's reasoning, that woman is subordinate to man.

4. The doctrine of angels argues for a covering (v. 10). Since our knowledge of angels is so extremely limited (cf. 6:3), it is not surprising that this puzzling passage has produced a multitude of interpretations. Perhaps it is best to understand it as having a bad influence upon angels, i.e., in the matter of throwing off proper authority. Or perhaps it is a simple admonition: You should do what is right because angels are watching.

5. A warning against a false inference (vv. 11, 12). These verses seem to be inserted in order to safeguard his teaching against the false interpretation that woman somehow is inferior. These verses indicate that she is not inferior, but only subordinate.

6. Their own good judgment argues for a covering (v. 13). Paul is confident he can trust the sensibility of the women themselves, so he puts the matter to them in a simple question: Is it proper that a woman pray to God uncovered? Of all the arguments Paul uses this is the only one which is based entirely on the social customs of the day.

7. The facts of nature argue for a covering (vv. 14, 15). Simply put, Paul is saying that nature itself has endowed women with a more ample covering in her hair. This argues the propriety of her being covered, and by extension also the propriety of an additional artificial covering.

How long should a woman's hair be? How long should a man's hair be? The answer must be a relative one, not an absolute. It cannot be stated in inches. It probably will vary greatly according to social practices. But in any case it is a shame for a man to wear his hair long like a woman. And for a woman to have her hair as short as a man's is a surrendering of a glory which should be hers. The notion that men in Bible times wore their hair long is erroneous, as verse 14 shows. As a matter of fact, pictures and statues of men of New Testament times (and we have many of them) show that men in those days wore their hair at least as short as the shorter hair cuts of today. Pictures of Christ which have fostered this notion had their origin in the imaginations of the artist rather than in historical information.

8. Universal custom of the churches argues for a covering (v. 16). The meaning is brought out well in the NASB, "If anyone is inclined to be contentious, we have no other practice, nor have the churches of God." If anyone is not satisfied from the arguments previously given, just remember the universal practice of the churches is for women to wear a covering.

II. PROPER CONDUCT AT THE LORD'S SUPPER (vv. 17-34)

Again, the subject under consideration is public worship, even more clearly stated than in the previous section. Note the words, "when you come together" (vv. 17, 18, 20, 34). Again, these matters are both referred to as ordinances which Paul has delivered to them (v. 2, 23). But in one respect there is a vast difference. With regard to the conduct of the women Paul's words were mostly praise (v. 2). In that matter their need was to be taught, "I would have you to know" (v. 3). Paul praises them for their commendable practice and wants only that they understand the meaning of the practice. But, with regard to this second topic of the chapter, by contrast, Paul's words are strong blame, "I praise you not" (v. 17).

The supper under consideration here, which was intended to be — but actually was not and could not be — the "Lord's supper," is the early Christian love-feast, the Agape. Instituted in the meal eaten by our Lord with His disciples in the upper room, it was practiced throughout the New Testament era (II Peter 2:13; Jude 12) as well as the post-biblical period of early church history, amply described by several of the church fathers. It was an ordinary meal eaten prior to and in connection with the observance of the eucharist, and is still practiced by many as part of a "threefold communion service." That this is not a reference to the eucharist alone is shown by the nature of the abuse (vv. 21, 33, 34). The eucharist is mentioned here also (vv. 23-30) to show the effect of their abuse of the supper that precedes it. They cannot eat and drink worthily after such a shameful supper.[5]

A. *Their Shameful Conduct* (vv. 17-22)

Paul uses very severe language in dealing with the abuses of the Lord's Supper. Their observance is actually harmful, rather than helpful (v. 17). It is evidence of schism and division in their midst (vv. 18, 19). Although they come together for the purpose of eating the Lord's Supper, actually their shameful practices make such a thing an impossibility. Instead of the Lord's Supper, it is their own supper (vv. 20, 21). The Lord's Supper was not intended to satisfy physical hunger. They can do that at home (v. 22). Although the Agape originally was a full regular meal with the entire congregation eating together, Paul makes it clear here that the purpose of that meal was not to provide physical food; rather, it was intended as a spiritual memorial. When, as at Corinth, the physical aspect of the meal

---

[5]An unfortunate confusion of terms warrants some explanations. The term "Lord's Supper," often incorrectly used to refer to the eucharist, occurs only here and refers properly to the common meal, the love-feast. It was called the *Lord's* Supper in specific contrast to one's own supper (v. 21). This was the Lord's Supper because He instituted it, and because its meaning centered completely in Him. The love-feast, or Agape, also refers to this common meal eaten before the eucharist. It was so called because of the mutual participation and concern which so characterized the early Christians. The term "eucharist," which derives from the Greek word for the giving of thanks, refers to the Bread and Cup, as instituted by our Lord. The term arose from the giving of thanks which accompanied their observance. The term "communion" (Greek, *koinōnia*) means "joint participation in something," "a sharing." Its scriptural usage is much broader, but it soon came to be used especially for that service in which the Christian signifies his partaking of and sharing in the benefits of Christ's death. Hence, the term "the communion service" has come to be used widely as a synonym for the eucharist. The "threefold communion service," as observed by the Brethren churches, consists of the love-feast and the eucharist, along with the washing of the saints' feet (John 13).

became exaggerated at the expense of the spiritual,[6] Paul admonished that they should do their eating to satisfy hunger in their homes before they came together for the Agape (cf. vv. 33, 34). For this reason many of those who observe the Agape today use only a token meal.

B. *Instruction Regarding the Eucharist* (vv. 23-26)

Paul received these instructions "of the Lord" (v. 23). When we compare this with 15:3 and Galatians 1:12, it appears that this detail also came to Paul directly from the Lord, not by communication from the apostles who had been present at the Last Supper. If this is the meaning intended, it adds greatly to the significance of the details here presented to know that the Lord Jesus saw fit to give them to the Apostle Paul by direct revelation.

Of the gospel accounts of this event, Luke's most closely resembles Paul's. It may well be that Luke has used Paul's revelation as his source here. Paul emphasizes that the bread and the cup are "in remembrance of" the Lord Jesus. In the light of this, their abuse of the love-feast is especially blameworthy. Since they had been eating their own supper instead of the Lord's, they were not in a proper attitude to partake of the emblems which remind them of Him. They were not doing it in remembrance of the Lord Jesus.

Verse 26 makes it clear that the bread and the cup were intended to be regularly observed by the Lord's people, "as oft as ye do it." This continuing practice thus becomes a constant proclaiming or publishing of the good news, a "visible word," a preaching of the entire church in silent ministry. Even in apostate churches where the message of the cross no longer is proclaimed from the pulpit, it may still be proclaimed from the

---

[6]Apparently it was the custom that these love-feasts were conducted after the manner which is today called "pot-luck," carry-in, or picnic dinners. Each family would bring a supply of food, the poor perhaps very little, and those who were able, more; then all would share together in the entire spread. But at Corinth, love was replaced by selfish greed. Each one hurriedly devoured his own supply without sharing. As a result, some were hungry and others were drunken.

table. Its message has a twofold direction. It looks backward to the Lord's death and forward "till he comes."

C. *Warning Regarding the Proper Manner of Participation* (vv. 27-32)

The extreme importance of this ordinance warrants a solemn warning against partaking in an unworthy manner.[7] What this unworthy manner is is made plain in verse 29. It is eating without discerning the Lord's body, eating without recognizing the symbolism which reminds of the Lord's body, without seeing Christ and His death in it all.

The warning leads to an admonition, the duty of self-examination. By judging, examining, or disciplining ourselves, we may avoid the Lord's disciplining. The word "damnation" in verse 29 should be read "condemnation," or "judgment." It is not talking about eternal damnation in hell, but a much more immediate judgment, the chastening hand of the Lord upon the believer for his sin (Heb. 12:5-11). Among such chastenings, Paul mentions physical sickness and even death (v. 30).

D. *Concluding Advice* (vv. 33-34)

Paul closes this section by repeating his admonitions on the observance of the Lord's Supper and a promise that he will straighten out the rest of their problems when he visits them.

Questions for Discussion

1. Is there another alternative as to what our attitude should be toward this scriptural teaching regarding the woman's head-covering?

2. Do verses 14 and 15 have anything to say regarding bobbed hair for women and shoulder-length hair for men today?

3. Are women inferior to men according to Paul? Would he endorse the modern Women's Liberation movement?

---

[7]The word "unworthily" (v. 27) is an adverb, not an adjective. He does not say, "If anyone *who is not worthy* partakes"; rather, he says, "If anyone partakes in an *unworthy manner*" (NASB). No one is worthy; but anyone may eat worthily, in the right manner.

4. What can you find in the Scriptures as to how often the communion service should be observed?

5. Does the abuse of the love-feast in Corinth justify the abandonment of its observance?

6. How can we make our communion observances more meaningful?

Chapter 9

ONE BODY — MANY MEMBERS

(12:1-31)

The formula which Paul uses to open this chapter suggests another matter about which they had written to him (cf. 7:1; 8:1). The spiritual gifts[1] referred to here are those supernatural, Spirit-bestowed endowments known to the early church, the "charismata," a word which has come into English by direct transliteration from the Greek. These are not natural abilities, such as musical talent, or the "gift of gab," or a natural-born salesmanship. A study of the lists of these Spirit-gifts as named in Scripture (see below) makes it clear that not one of them is related to a natural talent, and the arbitrary sovereign bestowal of these gifts by the Spirit on believers when they become a part of the body of Christ emphasizes this unnatural character. One might presume that the Holy Spirit would take into consideration natural abilities in distributing His supernatural gifts; but that would be human assumption, not scriptural statement. In fact, scriptural evidence in some cases indicates the opposite. Who would have thought that vacillating Peter would be picked for a rock? And the converted rabbinical student, Saul of Tarsus, would have been a "natural" to become an apostle to his own people; but the Spirit made him apostle to the Gentiles.

That the exercise of these grace-gifts had been a problem in the Corinthian church has been hinted at before in various places (e.g., 1:5, 7a). Their pride in knowledge and wisdom apparently reflected a fascination with the showier, more spectacular gifts. Their particular problem appears to have centered in the undue exaltation of tongues, as is shown repeatedly in

---

[1]In the original the noun modified by the adjective "spiritual" is left to be supplied. We may understand (1) men, (2) things or matters, or (3) from the context, gifts (cf. v. 4). Since the subject under discussion in this section is "spiritual gifts," the KJV is probably right in taking the third. The first two are quite general and foreign to the context.

this section. In Paul's listing of these gifts, he puts speaking in tongues at the end of the list (12:10). In his second listing he does the same (12:29, 30). He begins his chapter on love by relating it to the gift of tongues (13:1). Later in that chapter he makes a clear distinction between tongues and the other gifts in the way they will cease. And the whole of Chapter 14 is a discussion of this gift. Evidently the Corinthians had some problems with this particular gift. And it is not inappropriate to remark that this is the most problematic gift of all.

Paul treats this problem after the following outline: (1) A general presentation of the matter, the diversity of gifts and their function in the one body (chap. 12). (2) The one quality necessary to the exercise of any gift, i.e., love (chap. 13). (3) The specific problem at Corinth, the relative value of tongues and rules regarding their practice (chap. 14).

I. EVERY CHRISTIAN HAS THE SPIRIT (vv. 1-3)

Paul begins by reminding them of what every converted Corinthian knew, that the Spirit had been operating in their lives. Their conversion from paganism and their confession of Jesus proves it. Confessing the Lordship of Christ is impossible without the Spirit and such a confession is evidence of the possession of the Spirit. On the other hand, a denial of Christ can never come from one who possesses the Spirit.[2] It hardly needs to be said that these confessions spoken of in verse 3 involve more than pronouncing the words (cf. Matt. 7:21-23).

II. THE SOVEREIGN SPIRIT DISTRIBUTES HIS GIFTS TO EACH (vv. 4-11)

If the progression of thought seems to move abruptly from one idea to another, remember that this is an answer to a letter; we

---

[2]It may be that the words "Jesus accursed" (v. 3) had actually been spoken in the Corinthian church by someone professing to be "speaking by the Spirit" in tongue, as many commentators have suggested. If so, it was immediate and absolute proof that the speaking was *not* by the Spirit. What the Spirit says will always be in harmony with what He has said in the Scriptures. But such an inference is by no means certain.

have the answers but we do not have the questions. In this particular section, Paul seems to be demonstrating that the Holy Spirit has, in fact, bestowed grace-gifts on every believer.

A. *The Relation of the Trinity to Such Gifts* (vv. 4-6)

Each person of the Triune God has His own function in relation to these grace-gifts. There is a wide variety of them but the same Spirit is the giver of them all. There is a wide variety of ministries, or jobs (KJV, "administrations"), but the same Lord Jesus Christ is the "boss" (Lord) who directs the work to be done. There is a wide variety of accomplishments, or activities performed, but it is the same God, the Father, who accomplishes them all (cf. 3:7).

B. *The Purpose of the Gifts* (v. 7)

The "manifestation of the Spirit" here is the grace-gift which the Spirit gives. It is given to every man individually, but not for his personal enjoyment. The archaic expression of the KJV, "to profit withal," needs to be clarified; the purpose of the gift is "for the common good" (NASB). This idea will be developed in the figure of the body and its members. The Spirit gives to each member of the body that enablement which he needs to perform his particular function in that body, and for the good of the whole body.

C. *A Listing of the Gifts* (vv. 8-10)

Five places in the Scriptures we are given lists of these grace-gifts of the Spirit. Three are in this chapter (vv. 8-10; v. 28; and vv. 29-30). The other two are Romans 12:6-8 and Ephesians 4:11. It is strongly urged that the student should write down in parallel columns the list of gifts as given in each of these five places for the purpose of comparison.

Some observations may be made from this comparison. Sometimes these gifts are enablements, sometimes they are persons, sometimes they are offices. Sometimes they are official, sometimes private. Sometimes they are very specific, sometimes very general. Sometimes they are clearly defined, sometimes they are hard to determine. Some are temporary, others are permanent. Apostles and prophets and the confirmatory signs (cf. Heb. 2:4) belonged to the first century. Evangelists, pastor-teachers, exhorting, giving, ruling, and so on, belong to every age. No two lists are alike; in fact, only one gift finds a place in all of the lists. This would suggest that there is no well-defined list of these grace-gifts of the Spirit. Nor is there any indication in Scripture that the ones named in these five lists are intended to express all of the Spirit's gifts. Instead, we are led to conclude that the Spirit's gifts differ at different times and at different places according to needs.

D. *Each Christian Receives Such a Gift* (v. 11)

Here is another indication that the above list is not to be considered a complete and fixed listing of all the Spirit's gifts. For every Christian, without exception, receives one of His gifts. Which one of the eighteen or nineteen named in these five lists do *you* have? Of course, some of them, like helps, giving, showing mercy, are so general that they could be claimed by almost anyone. But verse 11 says that the Spirit gives to *every* one his *own* gift. Surely there must be more than eighteen or nineteen total functions needed in the operation of a complex body such as the church.

III. THE FIGURE OF THE BODY AND ITS MEMBERS (vv. 12-27)

A. *The Appropriateness of the Figure* (vv. 12-13)

This figure of speech[3] beautifully illustrates the lesson of diversity in unity which Paul wants to develop in the rest of this

---

[3]There is a significant development of this figure within the New Testament. Perhaps its beginning is to be found in the words of Christ to Paul on the Damascus Road, "Why are you persecuting *me?*" The one who touched the church was touching Christ. Here in I Corinthians and in Romans 12 the figure stresses the interdependence and importance of the members of the body. Of course, the head is not to be understood as that part of the body above the shoulders. The ear, the eye, and the nose are parts of the *body* not of the head. Rather, the head is that part of the body which directs and controls the rest, the one who gives the orders, the brain.

chapter. But it is more than an illustration. It is a figure representing a spiritual reality, a relationship actually existing between Christ and the believer through the functioning of the Holy Spirit.

This relationship is brought about by a baptism. Baptism in the New Testament is an initiatory rite, a symbolic ritual which introduces us into a new relationship. By this baptism, we are introduced into and become a member of the body of Christ, the church. The Spirit is not the baptizer[4] but the instrument or means of this baptism. When we receive the Spirit, "made to drink (i.e., partake) of the Spirit," we then possess the same life-giving Spirit that is in Christ. By receiving Him, we are identified with Christ and become part of His body.

B.   *The Lesson of Diversity* (vv. 14-19)

From this figure of speech the apostle draws two basic lessons. Verse 14 is the key to the first of these. There is one body but many members. In this section the emphasis is on the individual. The admonition is: Do not despise your own gift. Diversity is normal and needful to proper functioning of the body. The application of this principle means that the individual gift of each member, no matter how insignificant it may seem, is important to the body. Presumably, the Corinthians were exalting certain of the more spectacular gifts to the point that others felt that they had no gift at all, that they were not of the body. Paul's answer is that it takes many members to make a body.

C.   *The Lesson of Unity* (vv. 20-26)

The key to this corollary truth is verse 20. There are many members but only one body. Here the emphasis is on the unity. The admonition is: Do not despise another's gift. Their exalta-

---

[4]The KJV rendering, "by one Spirit," is misleading. This construction (Greek, *en*) is never used for the personal agent with a passive voice. The consistent representation of this doctrine of Spirit baptism in the New Testament is that Christ is the One who does the baptizing (Matt. 3:11; Luke 3:16; John 1:33; Acts 1:5), that He does this *in*, or with the instrumentality of, or by means of, the Holy Spirit. The historic occasion of that baptism on Pentecost was the receiving of that Spirit (Acts 2:38).

tion of certain gifts ignored the need of the one body for all the gifts (vv. 21, 22).

Especially is this true with respect to some of the seemingly insignificant parts of the body (vv. 23-25). These he describes as "more feeble" (better, "weaker"), "less honorable," "our uncomely [Greek, indecent] parts," reminding us that we bestow more abundant honor upon these parts by covering them with clothing. The reference here is obviously to the reproductive organs as being much more necessary, yet properly to be concealed. How different this is from the modern emphasis which often makes the reproductive process (so-called evangelism, soul-winning) as the most important, if not the sole function of the body, certainly the one most to be exposed.

IV. THE APPLICATION OF THIS TRUTH TO THE MATTER OF SPIRITUAL GIFTS (vv. 28-31)

Paul now presses home the lesson which he especially wants to draw from this figure of speech. The emphatic word in verse 28 is the word "some." God has put some of the Christians in the church to function as apostles, some as prophets, some as teachers, and so on. There is not a single one of these grace-gifts which is shared by every member of the church (vv. 29-30). In a series of rhetorical questions, asked in a form which indicates that he expected a negative answer, the Apostle Paul says, "Do all of you exercise the gift of an apostle? No, of course not." And on he goes through the list until he comes to the one which he wants especially to emphasize, "Do all speak with tongues, or interpret tongues? No, of course not."

In a real sense, verse 31 is the key to the whole passage. All the gifts are necessary, all are important, but some are greater than others and should be sought. Which are the best gifts? Look again at the list in verse 28. The first three are numbered, probably indicating the order of importance. Then follows an unnumbered miscellaneous list with tongues at the very end. The first two of those numbered are special gifts of the first century which are not present today. Of these primary gifts the teacher is the only one which is still in existence today. There is no higher gift in the church today than that of the pastor-teacher. Or, to get at the matter another way, from the context the best gift is that which benefits the most, that which edifies the church, that which contributes most to the common good of the body. This quality of edification will be the heart of Paul's discussion in Chapter 14.

"Covet earnestly [Greek, "be zealous for"] the best gifts." This admonition is not a contradiction of the truth presented earlier in the chapter, that the sovereign Spirit decides and bestows such gifts as He chooses. His sovereignty is not arbitrary. He may not give us the gift we ask for. But then again, He may. It is evidently His will to take into consideration our zealous desires; hence, this admonition.

Questions for Discussion

1. Is musical talent a gift of the Spirit?
2. From 12:1-3; Acts 19:1-2; 6:13; Romans 8:9 and many other Scriptures it appears that the possession of the Spirit was clearly recognizable, and an evidence of genuine salvation. Is the same true today? How?
3. What is the gift of faith (v. 9)?
4. What gifts of the Spirit are apt to be minimized in the church today?
5. What gifts of the Spirit are being over-emphasized or glorified in the church today?
6. What is *your* spiritual gift? You have one, you know.

View from Acrocorinth. Old Corinth at left, New Corinth in the middle distance, and isthmus and canal on the extreme right. Levant Photo

Chapter 10

LOVE IS THE GREATEST

(13:1-13)

I. A GEM AND ITS SETTING

"The greatest, strongest, deepest thing Paul ever wrote." Thus, one has described the chapter before us.[1] Many have called it St. Paul's hymn of love. "A lyrical interpretation of the Sermon on the Mount — the beatitudes set to music."[2]

A startling change takes place in the temper and style of the book at this point. Paul has been plodding through problem after problem with deep reasoning, carefully worded arguments, explanations, and warnings. "On each side of this chapter the tumult of argument and remonstrance still rages: but within it, all is calm, the sentences move in almost rhythmical beauty; the imagery unfolds itself in almost dramatic propriety; the language arranges itself with almost rhetorical accuracy. We can imagine how the Apostle's amanuensis must have paused, to look up in his master's face at the sudden change in the style of his dictation, and seen his countenance lighted up as it had been the face of an angel, as this vision of divine perfection passed before him."[3]

As a beautiful gem is set forth in greater brilliance by the setting chosen for it and in turn enhances that setting, so here. The context both throws light on and receives light from this beautiful gem. The context before and after is dealing with the

---

[1]Harnack, quoted in Archibald Robertson, "A Critical and Exegetical Commentary on the First Epistle of St. Paul to the Corinthians" in *International Critical Commentary,* ed. by Briggs *et al.,* Scribners, New York, 1916, p. 285.

[2]W. F. Howard, "First and Second Corinthians," *Abingdon Bible Commentary,* ed. F. C. Eiselen, *et al.,* Abingdon Press, New York, 1929, p. 1187.

[3]Arthur F. Stanley, *The Epistles of St. Paul to the Corinthians,* John Murray, London, 1876, p. 238.

grace-gifts, and particularly the gift of tongues. Chapter 12 introduces this subject as a problem in the Corinthian church. Chapter 14 is devoted entirely to a long discussion of the relative importance and the proper use of the gift of tongues. Inserted prominently between these, this great section on love also concerns itself with the same problem. "Though I speak with the tongues of men and angels . . . and though I have the gift of prophecy, and understand all mysteries, and all knowledge; and though I have all faith. . . ." All these are grace-gifts, a part of the setting of Paul's gem on love.

The chapter division is particularly unfortunate here because it tends to isolate this section from its context. Verse 31 of Chapter 12 serves as a transition and properly belongs to Chapter 13. Also the KJV translation is misleading here.[4] The meaning is better expressed by the ASV, ". . . and moreover a most excellent way show I to you." Paul is not saying that love is better than gifts, drawing a comparison between love and gifts. Rather, he is showing that love is the only way to make gifts effectual. The contrast is between gifts *with* love and gifts *without* love. "Though I speak . . . and have not love."

II. WHAT IS THIS LOVE?

The English word "love" cries out for definition. It is used in so many widely different senses that it needs careful explanation to be usable at all. Particularly in our day this is true, for it has become almost a "dirty word."

A. *What It Does Not Mean*

Love in this passage, and in the New Testament, never means romantic or sexual love. The Greeks had a word for that, but that word never appears in the New Testament. The emotions of lust and self-gratification which characterize so much of to-

---

[4]Greek, *kai eti*. The KJV "and yet" is possible grammatically but does not fit the context. The NASB connects *eti* with what follows, "and I show you a still more excellent way." The ASV, like the KJV, connects the *eti* with *kai* but understands it in the sense of, "and besides," "and moreover," adding to the exhortation just given "a way to carry it out." This last seems to express best the apostle's meaning.

day's love and love-making are almost the direct opposite of Biblical love. Even when the Scriptures admonish husbands to "love your wives" (Eph. 5:25) it is not talking about being more romantic (although that too may be needed), but it is speaking of another much needed quality.

Scriptural love does not mean a tingling sensation running up and down the spine in the presence of the one who is loved. In the common usage of the word today, it is almost always heavily loaded with the notions of feelings and sentimentalism; it is primarily an emotional word. Again this is almost the direct opposite of the scriptural sense. To demonstrate the truth of this statement, try to read this idea of emotional attraction into John 3:16!

Scriptural love is not merely a warm, friendly spirit of tolerance and "brotherhood." This so-called virtue, so highly acclaimed in religious circles today, often either reflects an unbelieving denial of the absolute verities of our Christian faith or is a selfish unwillingness to be concerned about the spiritual well-being of others, and actually shows a lack of love.

Scriptural love is not quite "charity," the word used by the KJV in this chapter. This word came into our English Bible from the Latin Vulgate. It has become greatly narrowed in meaning, until now it is used only in two senses: (1) giving to the poor, and (2) tolerance for differences of opinion. Originally the word had a broader meaning, signifying concern for the well-being of others, and action toward that end. If the word "charity" still carried that broader meaning, it would be a very good translation for "love" in this chapter.

B. *What It Does Mean*

The true meaning of Biblical love is to be seen, I believe, by noting its use in a couple of key passages: John 3:16 and I John 4:8-11. God has given a supreme example of what love means by what Christ did for us on the cross. His love was His concern for our deep need and His self-sacrificing action to benefit us. Our love is to be the same, a concern for the well-being of others, an active effort toward their benefit. It is not emotional but volitional. It is concerned not with how we feel but how we act. It responds not to the attractiveness of the other person but to the condition and need of the other person. Its motivation is not the selfish desire to enjoy the other person but the selfless desire to benefit him. Essentially, Christian love is concern and benevolence toward others.

That this is the true meaning of the word may be seen another way by comparing it with another Greek word found in the New Testament. *Phileō* does speak of love as a sentiment and emotion, a feeling: to be friendly, to be attracted to, to like someone. On the other hand the word here and most frequently in the New Testament (verb, *agapaō;* noun, *agapē*) is an action word; what we do and how we act toward others. These two words do not represent two different kinds of love,[5] but rather, two aspects of love. Both are usually present together.

III. AN INTERPRETIVE PARAPHRASE OF THE CHAPTER

The surpassing excellence of this passage makes one almost instinctively shrink back. To touch it is to spoil it. Yet, in spite of its beauty it comes to us in foreign dress and requires to be translated before its full beauty can be seen. It is the intent and hope of the present writer that he may be able in the following paraphrase to bring to mind some of the ideas and implications it would have conveyed to its original hearers. His aim is not beauty, but clarity and understanding.

[31]But in spite of the fact that spiritual gifts are gifts of the

---

[5]That these two words do not express two different types or kinds of love may be seen clearly by making a list of all the places in the New Testament where each of these words occur, noting the subjects and objects of each. The two lists will be almost identical, with a few instructive exceptions.

The often heard distinction that *phileō* refers to human love while *agapaō* refers to divine love cannot be supported from Scripture and introduces great confusion. Apparently drawn from such Scriptures as I John 4:7, 8 it is claimed that only born-again persons can exercise *agapē* love. But to the contrary, the Scripture often uses the word *agapaō* in describing the love of unsaved people (I John 1:15; John 3:19, etc.). This further illustrates that *agapē* love is not a different kind of love, but the concern and action aspect of love.

sovereign Spirit and differ to each member of Christ's body, it is still proper that you should desire and work zealously for the greater gifts (i.e., those which are more beneficial). And besides, I not only exhort you thus, I also point out to you a most excellent way of life; a way which must govern the exercise of all your gifts.

I. The Prominence of Love (vv. 1-3)[6]

[1]If ever I talk with the grace-gift of tongues, whether it be in human or angelic speech, and while I am so doing I am without that interest in and regard for the welfare of others that is supposed to be the peculiar possession of a Christian, I then have come to be in a state in which my wonderful gift amounts to no more than the noise made by pounding on a piece of brass or the shrill clanging of a cymbal. [2]And if I possess the gift of proclaiming divine truth in the authority of direct inspiration and, therefore, have understanding based on such perception of all divine secrets now released for explanation and of all other kinds of special knowledge; and if I possess in its entire extent this special grace-gift of exercising faith so that I could thereby be continually causing mountains to stand aside, and yet along with these marvelous spiritual possessions I do not possess that concern for the welfare of others that marked the life and ministry of our Lord Jesus Christ, then I amount to absolutely nothing. [3]And if I dole out all my property and distribute it in small portions to feed all the folks in need, and if I give my very body over to these needy ones as a sacrificial act of self-renunciation in order that I might have something to brag about in my acts of benevolence, and yet I do all these things without possessing that genuine interest in and concern for their welfare which should prompt such actions, I am benefiting myself not one bit.

II. The Properties of Love (vv. 4-7)

[4]Real love is patient, and slow to lose one's temper toward others who provoke us with injurious actions. It is quick to show kindness. It does not boil over with jealousy and envy. Love does not behave like a braggart, always "blowing off" like a windbag. It is not puffed up like a balloon with arrogance toward others. [5]It does not disgrace itself with indecency and shameful actions. It does not look out for Number One (its own affairs). It does not throw a tantrum and go into a fit of irritation when it is provoked. It does not keep careful account and mark down

---

[6]The outline is not my own but I do not know to whom credit is due.

against folks the evil things that they do against it. [6]It does not find cause for joy in the acts of wrong-doing it sees, but rather shares in the joy which truth experiences. [7]It bears up against everything. It shows faith in men and is not suspicious in all situations. It does not despair and always looks at the bright side of things. It perseveres in the face of every adverse circumstance.

III. The Permanence of Love (vv. 8-12)

[8]Love never falls into disuse. But if there be such things as prophesyings, they shall be put out of use; they shall give place to something else. If there be the speaking with tongues, they shall stop; they shall come to an end. If there be the gift of knowledge, it shall be put out of use; give place to something else. [9]For it is in partial piece-meal fashion that we presently exercise the gift of knowledge. It is in partial piece-meal fashion that we now prophesy. [10]But whenever the complete thing comes along then the partial is put out of use and replaced. [11]When I was a child I acted like a child in my speech, in my disposition, and in my reasoning and deciding. When I became a man I put the childish ways out of use and replaced them with adult ways. [12]For right now we see through the means of a mirror, and what we see is rather enigmatic, not too clear. But then, when the complete thing has come, we will exchange this mirror-sight for direct face-to-face sight. Now we know only in partial, piecemeal fashion. But then, when that perfection is reached, we shall know thoroughly even as we previously were thoroughly known by God.

IV. The Pre-eminence of Love (v. 13)

[13]And now, in conclusion, there are three things which stay and are permanent. Faith abides, hope abides, love abides. These three are permanent. But of these the greatest is love.

IV. TONGUES-SPEAKING IN THIS CHAPTER

The supremely excellent way characterized by the exercise of love has its application to the whole Corinthian situation, from their despising their leaders and forming hostile factions to their selfish disregard for the spiritual welfare of the weaker brethren. But especially is it brought to focus on their pride in spiritual gifts and their preoccupation with the tongues gift in particular. Not only in the context, but in the very heart of this most beautiful exposition of love, Paul relates it especially to the gift of tongues-speaking.

There is a difference to be noted in the way that Paul speaks of tongues as compared with prophecy and knowledge. Of course, all are equally ineffectual and useless if exercised without love (vv. 1-2). But when he speaks of their temporary nature, he makes a sharp distinction (vv. 8-10). This difference, unfortunately, is obscured by the KJV rendering. Speaking of both prophecy and knowledge, he uses a word (Greek, *katargeō*) which means "to be put out of use," "rendered inoperative." And the context makes it clear that this occurs by their being replaced with something better, "when that which is perfect is come." But when he speaks of tongues he uses a word (Greek, *pauō*) which means simply "to stop," "cease," "come to an end," with no indication that they are to be replaced, or that they serve a function which needs to be perpetuated by something better. Also, knowledge and prophecy continue under consideration in verses 9 and 10; whereas tongues simply drop out of consideration after verse 8.

Scripture apparently does not state explicitly the time when these gifts are to be replaced or terminate. However, two lines of scriptural teaching seem implicitly to determine it. First is the replacement of prophecy and knowledge by the coming of "that which is perfect." The present writer prefers the interpretation which sees this phrase as a reference to the completion of the New Testament Scriptures. The miracle gifts of prophecy and knowledge were invaluable to the early church, but they were always piecemeal, "in part" (Greek, *ek merous*). When, by the exercise of these oral gifts, the full canon of Scripture had been put into writing, the church then had a complete, perfect body of revelation, all they would need for their age and the ages to come. These temporary gifts then were replaced by that which is perfect. The usual interpretation, which refers the phrase to heaven or the second coming of Christ must either play down the miraculous, revelatory character of the gift of prophecy, or admit that such new revelation is going on today. Not many new books have been added to the Bible recently!

Second is the conclusion which may be drawn from the stated purpose of these miraculous grace-gifts. Hebrews 2:3 and 4 tells us that God used all these miracle gifts as a confirmation of the message of the apostles. It seems logical, therefore, that when this apostolic message had been committed to writing, the need for the supernatural gifts ceased. If it is objected that we still need confirmation for the written word, let attention be given to Luke 16:27-31. The inspired written word, the Scriptures, is self-authenticating.

As a matter of simple historical fact, these confirmatory miracle gifts *did* cease with the apostolic age. The apostleship ceased to exist. Prophets were replaced by teachers (cf. II Peter 2:1). The power to perform miraculous healings was diminishing even during the lifetime of the apostles (Phil. 2:25-30; I Tim. 5:23; II Tim. 4:20). Tongues are mentioned by none of the church fathers of the second century and were so completely unknown that later writers confess, in commenting on I Corinthians 12 to 14, that they no longer can understand what Paul is talking about. Thus Paul's prophecy was fulfilled; tongues ceased. The need for them ended when the writing of the New Testament was completed in the first century.

Questions for Discussion

1. When you tell an unbeliever today that God loves him, what will he understand you to mean?

2. Is love one of the spiritual gifts?

3. Are acts of humanitarianism done for unworthy motives really worthless?

4. Does love overlook faults?

5. Is there any connection between Paul's illustration of "growing up" in 13:11 and his reference to the Corinthian's childish fascination with the spectacular tongues-gift (14:20)?

6. In what way is love greater than faith? or hope?

Chapter 11

EVERYTHING MUST EDIFY

(14:1-40)

Paul has carefully prepared the way by showing that gifts are sovereignly given by the Spirit to each individual. They are for the benefit of all and are required to be exercised in love, i.e., in consideration of the good of others. Some gifts are better because they are more beneficial; these are the ones that should be sought after. Now he launches into a straightforward discussion of tongues, the subject of Chapter 14.

I. WHAT WAS THE GIFT OF TONGUES?

There are two main views: (1) that the gift of tongues was speaking in normal human languages, such as Greek, Hebrew, Latin, Russian, or English; (2) that the gift of tongues consisted of the utterance of unintelligible sounds, ecstatic speech. The cleavage between these two views is exceptionally sharp, and surprisingly it cuts across both groups, both those who accept and those who reject tongues-speaking as a valid gift of the present day. In this very brief treatment, rather than collecting and evaluating the arguments pro and con, I propose to look at the passage and try to draw some conclusions.

A. Two Determining Factors

In determining the nature of the gift of tongues as it was practiced in Corinth, two crucial considerations must be kept in mind.

1. The Corinthian Tongues Were Not Understood; They Were "Unknown" to Everyone Concerned

(a) Those who heard them did not understand them. This is the whole point of discussion in Chapter 14, "No man understandeth him" (v. 2). The tongues were unintelligible. Paul carefully explains throughout the chapter that in order to edify the church their utterances must be understood, and obviously the tongues were not. (b) Neither did the one who spoke understand them. On this point there is some disagreement, but a fair understanding of verse 13, "Pray that he may interpret," and verse 28, "If there be no interpreter, let him keep silence in the church," together with the argument in verses 14 to 19 that speaking in tongues was speaking apart from the understanding, seem to be decisive. No one, apart from a separate gift of interpretation,[1] understood the utterances of the tongues speaker. If we understand them as languages, it clearly means that they were unknown[2] languages, unknown to everyone involved. If

---

[1]Attempts have been made to understand the "interpretation" of tongues to mean "translation," and thus to argue for foreign languages. While the evidence is not absolutely decisive, it points rather to the opposite conclusion. Three Greek verb roots are involved, the simple *hermēneuō* and two compounds of it, *di-ermēneuō* and *meth-ermēneuō* together with their noun cognates. The last of these properly means "to translate" from one language to another. It is so used eight times in the New Testament, and never means anything else. This is *not* used by Paul in connection with the charismatic tongues. The other two words are both used in two senses: (1) to translate from one language to another (only three times, and only in explaining the meaning of a proper name), and (2) to explain, expound, interpret (used of Christ explaining the Old Testament Scriptures, Luke 24:27; cf. also its use by Plato to describe the interpretation of the inarticulate ravings of the mad oracle at Delphi). In this tongues context, Paul uses the words which normally mean "to interpret," "to explain the meaning of," and only rarely mean "to translate." He *never* uses the word which regularly means "to translate."

[2]It will be noted that "unknown" is in italics in the KJV, indicating that it is not in the original. Considerable objection has been raised against this insertion, by those who contend that the tongues are foreign languages, but to little point. If the charismatic tongues were *known* foreign languages, then 14:2 speaks nonsense: "He that speaketh in a known foreign language speaketh not to men, but to God." Even if it be granted that the gift did consist of speaking in actually existing foreign languages, these must have been unknown to all men present, known only to God.

Similarly another argument strongly pressed loses its significance, the argument that the word "tongue" or "tongues" when it does not refer to the physical organ, always refers to languages such as He-

tongues were ecstatic speaking, their unintelligible character would be obvious.

2. The Corinthian Tongues Were Being Abused

The second crucial characteristic of tongues-speaking at Corinth was that something was wrong with it. Here is a very important yet little understood factor in this problem. The gift of tongues in Corinth was being misused, and Paul wrote to correct and regulate its proper use. It was being rated too highly. It was being used excessively. It was contributing to disorder and confusion. Above all it was useless for edifying. But he makes no hint that it was spurious or pretended. Now the necessary implication is that it could not have been miraculous, in the sense that it was the direct working of God which enabled them to speak in tongues, else *God* was misusing His gift. If they could speak in tongues only as God gave them to speak, then when many of them caused confusion by speaking at one time it was really God causing the confusion by performing many miracles of speaking at one time; and so with the other abuses. If speaking in tongues was the ability to speak a foreign language not previously learned, then it was a miraculous power which could be performed only when God enabled, and could not be performed by more than one at a time unless God did it. It is simply impossible to conceive of the misuse of a totally miraculous gift. The conclusion seems inescapable: The gift of tongues was an ability which was capable of being used and controlled miraculously by God for His purposes, and was also capable of being used and controlled by the individual for unworthy and improper purposes. The problem at Corinth was the exercise of this gift in the power of the flesh instead of the power of God.

---

brew, Greek or Latin. It is agreed, of course, that such is frequently the case, but it was not always the case, as the present context illustrates. In 13:1 Paul speaks of the tongues of angels; was this Hebrew or Greek? Obviously it was *not* meant to refer to any known human language. It referred to language which conveyed meaning among angels. So in effect ecstatic speech conveyed meaning to God. It was a "language" of devotion.

B. *The Relation to the Pentecostal Gift*

Any consideration of the tongues phenomena in Corinth must also take into account the Pentecostal gift of tongues (Acts 2). It seems beyond question that they are both instances of the same gift. Paul wrote his letter to the Corinthians from Ephesus only a couple of years after the experience of tongues there (Acts 19:6) and it was only a few years later that Luke wrote his history, which unquestionably links the Ephesian tongues with those of Pentecost. The close connections of time and place require that the speaking of tongues in Corinth and at Pentecost be understood, in some measure at least, as the same gift.

Yet on the surface they appear to be drastically different. In Corinth Paul emphasized that not all spoke in tongues. Yet at Pentecost it is distinctly said that all spoke in tongues. At Corinth, the speaking was not understood. At Pentecost it was immediately understood. At Corinth it required interpretation. At Pentecost it made interpretation unnecessary. At Corinth it was addressed to God (14:2), at Pentecost, it is usually understood to have been addressed to men. At Corinth it was useless for evangelism; in fact, its effect was disastrous. At Pentecost 3,000 souls were saved. Little wonder that those with a low view of inspiration have concluded that Acts is confused here.

What is the solution? Several answers have been proposed. (1) They have been understood as two distinctly different gifts. This is highly improbable in the light of their close connection in Scripture. (2) They are two forms of the same gift. As pointed out before, the gifts of the Spirit are not to be thought of as hard and fast specific lists of precise gifts. Rather, they varied under different circumstances. Hence, the gift that was related to the "tongue" might on one occasion be ecstatic speech and on another occasion foreign languages. There is an element of truth in this but it does not go far enough.

(3) The third explanation claims that the gift of tongues always consisted of the miraculous speaking of unlearned foreign languages. This is widely held by many recent evangelical scholars, possibly because they believe it is more useful in refuting the modern tongues advocates. But in spite of prodigious

exegetical efforts it simply will not satisfactorily account for the situation at Corinth.

(4) A combination view seems preferable to the present writer.[3] The essential character of the gift was a deeply emotional outburst of praise and devotion to God, expressed in unintelligible, ecstatic speech. This was present at Pentecost also, as witnessed by the charge of drunkenness. But at Pentecost there was included also some measure of foreign languages which were immediately recognized and understood by those present. In their own dialects they heard "the wonderful works of God," i.e., ascriptions of praise and adoration. This foreign language speaking preceded Peter's sermon, and was not for the purpose of evangelism. Peter did not preach his Pentecost sermon "in tongue." Those present would all easily understand him speaking in Aramaic. Nor is there any record that the gift of tongues was ever used for evangelizing. The occurrence of well-known, easily recognized foreign languages in the tongues of Pentecost added to the wonder and the distinctive aspect of that unique event, the birthday of the church. Perhaps it was symbolic of the universal message of the gospel, and served as a fitting frontispiece for this "History of Christianity."

II. DEVELOPMENT OF PAUL'S ARGUMENT

A. *The Relative Value of Tongues* (vv. 1-20)

1. *Tongues and Prophecy Contrasted* (vv. 1-6)

Paul begins by picking up the thought of 12:31 (cf. 14:1), urging them to strive for the better gifts. Here he makes clear the basis of evaluation. Those are "better" which edify the whole church (vv. 3, 4, 5, 6, 12, 19). Judged on this standard prophecy is far better. In fact, tongues is well-nigh useless.

---

[3]This view was held by many older scholars and very recently has been ably elucidated and defended by Charles Russell Smith, *Biblical Conclusions Concerning Tongues* (unpublished doctoral dissertation, Grace Theological Seminary, 1970). It is to be hoped that this work will soon be published.

2. *The Necessity of "Understandability"* (vv. 6-17)

He states this point in verse 6. There is no profit to the church without understanding. He contrasts the results of coming to them with tongues and coming to them with revelation, or knowledge, or prophesying, or teaching (doctrine). The last-named list of four beneficial gifts all operate in the realm of the understanding.

Next he illustrates the principle (vv. 7-11), using two illustrations. (a) Musical instruments (he names three, the pipe or flute, the harp, and the war trumpet) illustrate the uselessness of that which is not understood. Such instruments make inarticulate sounds. Unless we are able to distinguish the tune, or the mood, or the message, or the action intended, unless we understand its meaning, it has no value.

(b) His second illustration involves speaking in foreign languages. This illustration gets even closer. Foreign languages do have significance in themselves (in contrast to musical instruments), but even so they are profitless, not edifying, unless they are understood by those who hear. The use of foreign languages as an *illustration* of an aspect of tongues seems to make it clear that the tongues in Corinth were *not* foreign languages. One does not compare things that are identical, nor illustrate a point by restating the point.

Paul insists that edification requires the exercise of the understanding (vv. 12-17). So speaking in a tongue requires an interpretation (v. 13), since in exercising this gift, whether by speaking or praying or singing, the spirit only is involved. But in church,[4] the requirement of mutual edification demands that both the spirit and the understanding must be active (vv. 14-17).

3. *Paul's Own Estimate of Their Value* (vv. 18-19)

It may surprise us to read that Paul spoke in tongues, but it should not. He was an apostle and exercised the signs of an apostle. He was present in Ephesus when they spoke with tongues. Yet his evaluation of the gift may be seen, negatively,

---

[4]The church, of course, is the assembly of believers, not the building.

in that he never mentions it anywhere else and here he gives it a five-to-ten-thousand rating.[5] Again, it is hard to conceive Paul's making such a statement as this if the Corinthian tongues were foreign languages.

4. An Appeal to Good Sense (v. 20)

The reference to childishness and maturity in this context is illuminating. This church which prided itself on its wisdom and intellectual enlightment, was, in the matter of tongues, showing a childish[6] fascination for a gift which appealed to their love for personal display, rather than their love for the benefit of the church.

B. Tongues as a Sign (vv. 21-25)

Here is a most difficult section to think through. It is easier to tell what it does not mean than to say precisely what it does mean. (1) Of course, it does not mean that tongues are a sign of the baptism of the Holy Spirit. They are a sign to the unbeliever, not to the believer. (2) The interpretation which makes tongues-speaking the fulfillment of a prophecy quoted from Isaiah 28:11-12, a judicial sign of confirmed unbelief, like the use of parables in Matthew 13, has been commonly held. But it is beset with many difficulties, such as the unquestioned literal meaning and fulfillment of the Isaiah prophecy, the fact that those who spoke in tongues were not always Gentiles, and especially the fact that unbelieving Jews are not prominent in any of the occurrences of tongues-speaking in the New Testament (in half the cases there were not even any unbelieving Jews present). This view appears to have its strongest impetus in the desire to prove that tongues-speaking was in foreign languages. (3) Perhaps the simplest view is to understand the word "sign"

---

[5]This should not be understood as a numerical comparison. The Greek word *myrioi*, translated "10,000" is the largest number in the Greek language which has a name and hence came to be used in an indefinite sense for "innumerable," "countless" (cf. English, myriads).

[6]"It is indeed the characteristic of the child to prefer the amusing to the useful, the brilliant to the solid." F. Godet, *Commentary on the First Epistle of St. Paul to the Corinthians,* tr. Rev. A. Cusins, Grand Rapids, Zondervan, 1957, vol. II, p. 287.

in its simplest meaning, "an indication of." The passage would then mean: Tongues signify something to the unbeliever. They are an indication to him that the tongues-speaker is mad. On the other hand, prophecy is an indication that God is with the believer.[7] Paul has been showing that tongues-speaking is wholly unprofitable to the believers in the church assembly. Here he makes it clear that speaking in tongues is also unprofitable in the work of evangelism.

C. *Regulations for the Exercise of Tongues* (vv. 26-40)

The situation at Corinth was such that Paul needed to regulate the use of this gift by laying down certain rules.

1. The first is a general one, "Let all things be done unto edifying" (v. 26). The word "all" is emphatic. When the brethren come together *everything without exception* must contribute to the edification of the saints.

2. Only two, or at the most three, are to speak in any one service (v. 21). Later, in verse 29, he applies the same rule to the gift of prophecy.

3. Each is to speak in turn (i.e., one after the other; "that by course," v. 27).

4. The interpretation must be given, otherwise the speaker must keep silent (vv. 27-28). Lest someone should reason that verse 28 merely requires the presence of an interpreter, please note that the last of verse 27 requires that in every case the interpretation actually be given.

Verses 29 to 32 simply remind us that the requirement of edification applies to the exercise of the gift of prophecy as well. Verse 32 is especially significant. The one who exercised the gift of prophecy, and also by implication the gift of tongues, was not overwhelmed by a compulsive external power which moved him automatically without his control. Rather, he was able to speak, or to wait his turn, or to refrain from speaking. In accordance with the regulations here stated, he knew what he was doing and was responsible for his actions.

---

[7]A full development of this interpretation may be seen in Timothy H. Farner, *1 Corinthians 14:21 — Paul's Use of Isaiah 28:11, 12* (an unpublished critical monograph, Grace Theological Seminary, 1967).

5. "Let your women keep silence in the churches" (vv. 34-35). The context here suggests strongly that this prohibition applies specifically and only to speaking in tongues.

6. The exercise of tongues must always be subservient to the authority of the written word of God: "If any man think himself to be . . . spiritual, let him acknowledge that the things that I write unto you are the commandments of the Lord" (vv. 36-38). The same Spirit who moved the tongues-speaker also moved Paul and the other writers of Scripture. Hence every utterance of the tongues-speaker must be in harmony with the Word of God, not adding to nor taking away from it.

7. "Let all things be done decently and in order" (vv. 33, 40). God is not the author of confusion, nor of indecency, impropriety, and disorder. Paul must have been trying to picture in his mind what the public services in Corinth were like (cf. v. 26) when he wrote this rule. The fact that it was necessary to make these regulations reflects on the sad spiritual condition of the church in Corinth.

III. SOME CONCLUDING OBSERVATIONS

We have not been able to deal adequately with this important subject, or with this chapter. Perhaps a few brief statements may summarize our understanding of it.

The *form* of the gift of tongues was an emotional outburst of praise and adoration in unintelligible ecstatic speech.

The *purpose* of the gift of tongues was primarily confirmatory (cf. discussion on 13:6 and Heb. 2:3-4). When that purpose was fulfilled, it ceased. If this gift should recur in the present time it would be serving a different function and would, therefore, be essentially a different gift.

The *side-effect*, or secondary function, was personal, private edification (edification in the sense of "a spiritual lift," not in the sense of instructional or informational growth). After the gift had ceased in the church this secondary benefit would be carried on by praying and singing with the spirit and with the understanding also (vv. 14-19; Eph. 5:18-20).

As Paul's statements here indicate, the gift of tongues was *of minimal importance* in the early church, perhaps the least of all gifts. Besides here, tongues are mentioned on three occasions in the book of Acts (chaps. 2, 10, 19) and nowhere else in the Bible. They were not a mark of high spirituality. They were prominent in the Corinthian church, which was a "problem church" spiritually. In each of the Acts incidents they were associated with new Christians. If tongues should recur today they would be required scripturally to conform to every one of these regulations listed by Paul. This consideration alone is sufficient to disqualify the vast majority of modern tongues advocates.

If modern tongues is not the genuine gift of tongues as practiced in the early church, then what is it? Some would say that it is of Satan, or demons. And perhaps this is true in some rare instances. The present writer has observed some manifestations which fearfully suggested it. But certainly not all modern tongues advocates are demon-possessed. Many of them are devout Christians who love the Lord. However, even in such cases, Satan, by deluding the believer, may be using it for his own ends. It is my conviction that the vast majority of modern tongues is a work of the flesh, a highly emotional, psychologically-induced frenzy in childish, immature Christians, seeking to imitate in the flesh the spiritual experience of the early church.

Questions for Discussion

1. How many ways can you think of that the tongues-speaking in Corinthians and in Acts 2 are alike? That they are different?

2. Is there any indication in the Scriptures that the miraculous gift of healing ever was, or could be, misused?

3. In what sense did tongues edify the one who spoke them (v. 4)?

4. What useful functions did the gift of tongues serve in the early church? Do the modern advocates of tongues-speaking claim these same functions?

5. Since the Bible was completed has God ever given any new truth to men through prophecy or tongues?

6. Do modern tongues advocates "keep the rules" laid down here?

Propylaea. Gateway from Lechaeum Road to Agora, Bema tribunal in center, and Acrocorinth in background. Levant Photo Service.

Chapter 12

WHAT WE LOOK FORWARD TO

(15:1-58)

This doctrinally important chapter on the resurrection is thrust before us by Paul without explaining why. Perhaps it is a demonstration of the edifying results which are produced by prophecy (cf. chap. 14). More probably it was introduced because there were problems about it in the Corinthian church (cf. vv. 12, 35). It is not clear how Paul learned of these problems. It comes in that section of the book where Paul has been answering problems communicated by official letter. But it does not begin with the customary phrase. Perhaps their letter had betrayed some questionings on the part of some, and Paul, knowing the seriousness and importance of the matter, volunteered answers they had not asked for.

It is not strange that questions about the resurrection should arise in Greek Corinth. Resurrection was a strange, almost inconceivable notion to the Greek mind. This was seen in what happened when Paul preached at Athens (Acts 17:18). The Greek philosophers described the content of Paul's message as being a "setting forth of strange gods . . . Jesus and the resurrection," where "Resurrection" (Greek, *anastasis*) appears to be one of Paul's strange gods.[1] At the end of his Mars Hill discourse the reaction is described, "When they heard of the resurrection of the dead some mocked" (v. 32). The word "mocked" means "scorned," "ridiculed." Platonism, with its notion that the body is the temporary prison of the soul and that the soul alone is immortal, had no place in its thinking for a doctrine of resurrection.

It must be made clear here at the start, because there has been much foolish and unscriptural teaching on this point, that the resurrection is a term which has to do with the *body*. It has nothing to do with the "immortality of the soul," or the persis-

---

[1] This interpretation is reflected in the translation of NEB.

tence of existence beyond the grave. It is the doctrine that a man "stands up" (Greek, *anastasis*) again after he dies, he comes back to life in the body. While the term is used in the Scriptures in a metaphorical sense of a spiritual resurrection, this too is not persistence of the soul. It is coming back to life again (spiritually) in regeneration.

I. THE GOSPEL CONFESSION OF THE RESURRECTION (vv. 1-11)

Here we have our oldest written account of the resurrection of Christ, antedating by many years the four gospel records and the Acts. It is particularly significant when we realize that Paul apparently claims to have received this message directly from the Lord himself, rather than through historical witnesses (v. 3, cf. 11:23 and Gal. 1:11-12).

Paul introduces the subject by solemnly declaring it to be one of the two major dogmas of the Christian gospel. This is Paul's only formal statement of the content of the gospel message. The good news by which they have been saved consists of two historic facts, Christ's death and resurrection, and their explanation and interpretation "according to the scriptures." The first of these historic facts, that Christ died, was proved by His burial. The second historic fact, that he rose again the third day, was proved by His being seen (by many groups listed in vv. 5-9). But these historic facts alone, certainly not the first one, are not in themselves the good news. They become "gospel" when it is realized that Christ died "for our sins, according to the scriptures." It is the scripturally interpreted significance of those historic events which constitute the good news.

This definition of the content of the gospel is consistent with apostolic preaching and New Testament teaching elsewhere. It was Peter's message on Pentecost, and Paul's message on Mars Hill. It is the theme of the book of Romans, where Paul makes it clear that the death and resurrection of Christ is the basis not only of justification (Rom. 4:25), our *past* salvation from the *penalty* of sin, but also the secret of sanctification (Rom. 6:1-11), our *present* salvation from the *power* of sin, and ultimately our glorification (Rom. 8:11, 17-19), our *future* salvation from the very *presence* of sin.

II. THE DISASTROUS DENIAL OF THE RESURRECTION (vv. 12-19)

In spite of the importance of the doctrine of the resurrection of Christ, there were those in the Corinthian church who were denying the possibility of a resurrection (v. 12). Probably they were not denying the historical fact of *Christ's* resurrection, they were willing to accept that as a strange and unusual fact pertaining to a very unusual Person. Yet they were saying there is no such thing as a resurrection of the *Christian's* body. Perhaps this was a part of their Greek "intellectuality." Paul's argument is logical and forceful. (1) If you deny resurrection in general, then by implication you deny Christ's resurrection (vv. 12-13), and (2) if you deny Christ's resurrection you deny the whole gospel message, with all its benefits (vv. 14-19).

III. THE UNIVERSAL EFFECT OF THE RESURRECTION (vv. 20-22)

Having shown the futility and utter hopelessness involved in the denial of the resurrection, Paul now confidently reasserts his conviction of its truth and draws from it a precious consequence. Christ's resurrection was not an exception, it was a guarantee. Again he alludes to the Jewish passover and its symbolism (cf. 5:7-8). Part of the ritual of that festival was the offering of the "sheaf of the first-fruits . . . on the morrow after the sabbath" (Lev. 23:10-11). This offering of the first-fruits was a pledge of the rest of the harvest. So Christ, whose resurrection occurred on the very day of the offering of the first-fruits, is by His resurrection a pledge and guarantee that others will follow.

Again, he argues the same point by the analogy of Adam as a type of Christ (cf. Rom. 5:12-21). As through Adam death came to all men, so through Christ life will come to all men.[2]

---

[2]Whether the "all" who are made alive in Christ includes all who died in Adam depends upon the meaning given to the words "made alive." If they mean "made spiritually alive"; then the "all" must be

IV. THE SEQUENCE OF THE RESURRECTION (vv. 23-28)

In this remarkable passage, more clearly than anywhere else in Scripture, Paul outlines the chronological order of the resurrection of all men. Observe carefully that all men are to be raised, but not all at the same time; "every man in his own order." The Bible knows nothing of one future general resurrection. Instead, the resurrections proceed in well-defined stages.

The first stage was the resurrection of Christ himself, "Christ the first-fruits." Since the first-fruits offering was not a single grain but a sheaf, it is possible that the first-fruits resurrection here mentioned may include others, perhaps that mysterious group in Matthew 27:52-53.

The next stage of the resurrection includes the saved, "they that are Christ's," and comes later, "afterward . . . at His coming" (v. 23). The time referred to (Greek, *parousia*) is a broad term which may refer to both aspects of the second advent of Christ. "They that are Christ's" also is a broad term intended to include all the saved of all ages. This stage of the resurrection, therefore, is the one which Jesus called "the resurrection of life" (John 5:29). John, in Revelation 20:5, calls it "the first resurrection." It thus includes at least three groups of the saved: (1) the church, to be resurrected and raptured at the beginning of the tribulation period (vv. 51-52; I Thess. 4:16-17); (2) the Old Testament saints, who, according to Daniel 12:1-2, are to be raised at the end of the tribulation period; (3) the tribulation saints, to be raised at the end of the tribulation period (Rev. 20:4-5). No further resurrection of saints will be needed from that time on; never again will death come to any of God's saints.

The character of the resurrection involved in the third stage is not so explicitly described in this passage, but the time is made clear; "then cometh the end," further identified as the time when the millennial, mediatorial kingdom of Christ will come to an end and will be incorporated into the eternal kingdom of God

---

taken as "all who are in Christ." But that expression can just as well mean "to bring to life physically," "to resurrect from the dead." The Bible does teach the resurrection of all men, both saved and lost (John 5:28-29; Rev. 20:5-6). Also the context in this passage (vv. 23-28) seems to be a listing in order of all the resurrections.

the Father in the eternal state. This is precisely the time described in Revelation 20:11 to 15 when "the rest of the dead,"
i.e., those who were not included in the first resurrection, and
therefore all the unsaved dead, will be raised to stand before
the Great White Throne judgment. Jesus called this "the resurrection of condemnation" (John 5:29).

V. THE INCENTIVE OF THE RESURRECTION (vv. 29-34)

There follows further illustration of the consequences of denying the resurrection, a continuation of the thought of verses 12
to 19. This time he shows the tragic effects of removing the
powerful incentive of the resurrection from the Christian conduct and service. He applies it in three areas:

1. The hope of the resurrection as held by saved people was
after they died a powerful incentive to their unsaved loved-ones
still living to be saved and baptized (v. 29).[3] If the dead do not
rise, the desire to rejoin saved loved ones who have passed away
would no longer lead men to come to Christ and be baptized.

2. The confidence of a future resurrection has been a powerful incentive to personal endurance and suffering for the cause of
Christ (vv. 30-32). Without a resurrection, what motive could
justify constant danger and suffering for Christ? Paul uses himself as an example. To "stand in jeopardy" is "to be in danger."
His claim in verse 31, "I die daily" means that he daily risked
death; he put his life on the line. His reference in verse 32 to
fighting with beasts at Ephesus is probably not to be taken literally. There is no record of his having done so; as a Roman citi-
zen he would be exempt from such treatment, and he makes no
mention of this in his list of sufferings in II Corinthians 11:23-
28. Rather, the expression is to be understood in a figurative
manner. In Ephesus he had contended with opponents who
were fierce as beasts. There would be no reason for such suf-

---

[3]This is admittedly a very difficult passage. Someone has counted
over 40 different interpretations! The one reflected above seems to be
the happiest solution in the light of our present knowledge. It is the
view presented by Herman A. Hoyt, unpublished mimeographed class
notes on I Corinthians, Grace Theological Seminary.

fering if there were no resurrection. If the dead are not raised, then eat, drink, and die.

3. The assurance of resurrection has been a powerful incentive to right conduct. Here Paul quotes a line of Greek poetry, known to us from the comic dramatist Menander, but probably a proverbial saying widely quoted: "Bad company corrupts good morals" (NASB). It is a warning from Paul that wrong doctrine produces wrong living. Association with those who were denying the resurrection would corrupt the moral principles and practices of the Christians at Corinth. Indeed, Paul already in this epistle has called attention to this danger (cf. 6:13-14). Verse 34 is an admonition to sober thinking. They have among them some who demonstrate a willful refusal to know the truth about God. This is a situation for which they ought to be thoroughly ashamed.

VI. THE "HOW?" OF THE RESURRECTION (vv. 35-41)

The thought turns now from the fact of the resurrection to its manner. Verse 35 is a key to the section which follows. It poses two questions: How? (to be answered in vv. 36-41) and, With what body? (to be answered in vv. 42-49). These questions apparently reflect, not the wonder of an honest seeker after the truth, but the questionings of those deniers of the resurrection who were seeking to show that it was unreasonable. Paul's address in verse 36, "thou fool," suggests one who "isn't using his head." If he would just think about it he would find his answers in his own experience. Paul begins by using the analogy of new life springing forth from seed that is sown in the ground, and from this draws out several lessons.

1. There can be no new life until the seed has died (v. 36). Jesus used this same analogy in John 12:24. Perhaps these deniers of the resurrection in Corinth were attempting to spiritualize its meaning, making it something which the Corinthians already possessed. Paul's answer is: No resurrection until after death.

2. We may expect resurrection to result in a change (v. 37). We sow a bare grain of wheat but what comes up is more and different (probably a reference to the new stalk).

3. In spite of the change it is still the same (vv. 38-39). Its identity will be preserved; "to every seed his own body." If this should seem difficult, Paul turns to another analogy, the wonderful diversity of bodies which God has produced in His world, a particular kind for every variety of being.

4. The new body will be suited to the new conditions (vv. 40-41). In listing the various kinds of bodies which there are, Paul moves from the lower realm of seeds, through flesh, and on to the celestial bodies. Later he will return to these as characterizing the type of body that will be suited to our resurrection.

VII. THE BODY OF THE RESURRECTION (vv. 42-49)

In response to the second question of verse 35, "With what body do they come?" Paul gives a series of five contrasts, showing their condition "before and after" the experience of death and resurrection. (1) Corruption changes to incorruption. This word does not carry our notion of "corrupt" or "evil." Rather it means "incapable of decay or destruction," "imperishable," a close synonym of "immortal." (2) Dishonor is exchanged for glory. (3) Weakness will give place to power; better, sickness will be replaced by strength. (4) The natural body will be replaced by a spiritual body. The body which we now have is one suited to life on the level of the soul, the *psyche* (cf. 2:14). But the resurrection body will be one suited to life lived on the level of the spirit. "Spiritual" does not mean "immaterial," "intangible," "ghost-like," as opposed to material. He does not say it will be a spirit; he says it will be a spiritual body. (5) The earthy will give place to the heavenly body. Our present body is of the earth and suited to habitation on the earth. Our resurrection body will be fashioned after the pattern of the Lord from heaven, and suited to a life in heaven.

Here, as in Romans 5:12-21, Paul makes a typological connection between Adam and Christ. In the Romans passage this connection is seen in their respective relationships to sin. Here he draws a comparison in their relationships to our bodies. From Adam we received our present, natural bodies. From Christ, by way of resurrection, we shall receive our spiritual, heavenly bodies. Christ, the last Adam, was made a quickening Spirit when He was raised from the dead (cf. Rom. 1:4; 6:4, and especially the whole context here. Before resurrection He too had a natural body). Thus Paul leads us to the most instructive illustration of all to teach us what the resurrection body will be like. "We shall also bear the image of the heavenly" (v. 49). He will "change our vile body, that it may be fashioned like unto His glorious body" (Phil. 3:21). What was His resurrection body like? "We shall be like Him" (I John 3:2). Meditate on that, and rejoice!

VIII. THE MYSTERY OF THE RESURRECTION (vv. 50-53)

In scriptural language a mystery is not something mysterious or hard to understand. It is something that has to be revealed. Now Paul lets us in on a secret, a truth which could not be reasoned out and which up to this moment had never before been revealed. "We shall not all sleep" (a euphemism for death); we shall not all die.

Paul had already revealed to the Thessalonians that those who had fallen asleep in Jesus would not miss the blessings of the second coming of Christ (I Thess. 4:13-18). When the Lord in His coming descends from heaven with the trump of God, then "the dead in Christ shall rise first," and "we which are alive and remain shall be caught up together with them . . . to meet the Lord in the air." In that passage he had said nothing about the condition of those who were alive and remained when they went up. Now in this Corinthian passage he explains what will happen. Before these saints, living in their present natural bodies, are ready to be taken up a change must take place. "Flesh and blood cannot inherit the Kingdom of God. . . . Corruptible must put on incorruption . . . mortality must put on immortality. . . . The dead shall be raised incorruptible and we shall be changed." So here is the secret: A whole generation of believers, who will still be living in their natural bodies at the time of the Rapture, will experience an instantaneous transformation by which they receive their glorified resurrection bodies, without dying.

IX. THE VICTORY OF THE RESURRECTION (vv. 54-57)

Paul sees resurrection, and the resurrection body, as the ultimate victory over man's greatest enemy, death. The hurt and pain of death, of course, is in its punitive character. Death is the consequence of sin, aggravated as well as revealed by the law. But resurrection is the undoing, the reversal, of death. As he contemplates this, Paul appropriates the language of the Old Testament and bursts forth in an expression of praise to God for the victory over death made possible through our Lord Jesus Christ.

X. THE APPLICATION OF THE RESURRECTION (v. 58)

This truth of the resurrection is not just a theoretical doctrine to be contemplated and adored. Paul closes this wonderful chapter by a practical application. Since you are going to be raised again from death, your labor is not in vain in the Lord. Therefore, you should (1) stand true, "steadfast, unmovable" and (2) work hard, "always abounding in the work of the Lord."

Questions for Discussion

1. Is the resurrection of the body universally accepted by all Christians today?

2. Can a person be saved who rejects the doctrine of Christ's bodily resurrection?

3. Did Paul ever see Christ, literally?

4. How many resurrections will there be? Tell when each will take place, and who will be included in each.

5. What can we learn about the nature of our resurrection bodies by studying the actions of Christ in his resurrection appearances?

6. When the Rapture occurs, what will be our first inkling of it?

Chapter 13

SOCIAL CONCERNS

(16:1-24)

"Now concerning the collection. . . ." So Paul begins a brief treatment of the last question in their letter. He will have more to say about it in a later letter (II Cor. 8—9). The Corinthians, of course, were familiar with the project from earlier instruction, and he does not say enough about it here to identify it for us, but by comparing other Scriptures we can learn what it was.

The Christian believers at Jerusalem were poor. This was witnessed to by the sharing of goods in Acts 4 and 5. The condition evidently continued for a long time, perhaps because Jerusalem was the center of Jewish antagonism to the gospel. Paul had been involved before in an offering to relieve that poverty (Acts 11:27-30). The Jewish leaders had requested of Paul and the Gentile churches that they remember the poor (Gal. 2:10). Now on the third missionary journey Paul was making this a special concern. The project was already under way in Galatia (v. 1). The Macedonians had taken to it enthusiastically (II Cor. 8, 9) and evidently the Corinthians had written to Paul about it. Later, when the project was completed, Paul gratefully mentioned its purpose and his hopes for it in his letter to Rome (15: 25-32). He proudly delivered it to Jerusalem in what he hoped would be a gesture of good will from his Gentile churches to their Jewish brethren.

Poverty was one of the social evils prevalent in the world of of that day. There were many others: slavery, materialism, immorality, disease, violence, drugs, discrimination, and more. Paul's gospel was not a "social gospel" in the modern sense of that term, but it was aware of, and concerned for, these problems. Paul, like his Master before him, was not a social reformer, He led no crusade for the abolition of slavery. But he preached a gospel which wiped out the distinction between slave and master, making them both brothers in Christ. And that basic spiritual and social doctrine ultimately has brought to an end the

institution of human slavery. Not in all of the social evils has the
gospel been so successful, but Bible-believing Christians have
been in the vanguard of most movements for human betterment.
The example of the early church's concern for the poor in Jerusalem shows the basic gospel method: (1) they cared, (2) they
shared.

His instructions here have to do with the manner of collecting
the money. To avoid a frantic drive to gather it together when
he arrived, he advised that each should lay aside each week according to the measure of prosperity God afforded him. The collection was to be made (1) individually and universally, "each
one"; (2) regularly, "on the first day of the week"; (3) sys-
tematically, "lay by him in store," i.e., to put it aside and ac-
cumulate it as a treasure; (4) proportionately, "as God hath
prospered him."

This mention of the first day of the week needs special com-
ment. Why that particular day? Evidently it was a day of
special significance to the Christians, the day when they met
together as a church. The term "the Lord's Day" is not known to
have been used until much later (Rev. 1:10), but there is ample
indication in the Scriptures themselves that the first day of the
week was thought of as pre-eminently the day that pertained to
the Lord Jesus Christ, the day of His resurrection. The first
gatherings of the believers were held on that day (John 20:19,
26). Pentecost, the birth-day of the church, came on the first
day of the week. The early Christians did not observe the sabbath day (Col. 2:16), evidently understanding that it was a part
of the old covenant law which had been abrogated by Christ,
along with sacrifices and laws of clean and unclean food. It is
the only one of the ten commandments which is not repeated
in the New Testament. But the Christians did obviously come
together in public services, and what more natural choice for
that time of meeting than the day which celebrated their Lord's
resurrection? This is remarkably confirmed by a study of Acts
20. There Paul was hurrying to get from Corinth to Jerusalem
by Pentecost (20:16). He left Philippi just after Passover (20:6)
and in five days sailing he arrived at Troas. But strangely, in
spite of the hurry, the record says they abode seven days at
Troas. Why? The next verse answers, "And upon the first day of

the week when the disciples came together to break bread"
(20:7). Paul and his party evidently had arrived in Troas on
Monday morning. Their only opportunity to meet with the
brethren demanded that they wait until the following Sunday,
which was the usual time for their gathering. Then on the
evening of the first day of the week, Paul met with them in a
long service (which included the interesting story of Eutychus)
and continued until daybreak (v. 11). Immediately the next
day they hurriedly continued their journey (vv. 13-14). So we
have ample evidence that from the very first the early church
observed the first day of the week as their special day of worship.

In verses 3 and 4 Paul gives some interesting instructions as
to how this offering is to be handled. The church was to select
men whom they approved as trustworthy to care for the money.
Official letters of recommendation authorizing these men to act
in this capacity were to be given. These, together with similar
delegates from other churches who had shared in the offering,
were to accompany Paul to Jerusalem to deliver the funds. Acts
20:1-4 lists many of these representatives of Gentile churches
who journeyed with Paul on that occasion. The significance of
this provision is far reaching. Where the handling of money is
involved Christians should take every precaution to secure trustworthy and honest men and to use business-like methods of
procedure. Paul did not want to allow any occasion for scandal
by handling the matter himself.

II. TRAVELING PLANS (vv. 9-12)

The body of the letter now finished, Paul closes with some
personal plans, a few greetings, and some closing admonitions.
Earlier (4:19, 21) he had threatened to pay them a visit. Now
in closing he explains his plans (vv. 5-9). He is going to stay at
Ephesus until Pentecost, for a great opportunity of preaching
the gospel is open to him there and there are many who op-
pose him. After Pentecost he wants to spend the summer
evangelizing in Macedonia, then he plans to come to Corinth and
spend the winter with them there. He could perhaps visit them
very briefly on his way to Macedonia, but he prefers to make his
next visit a longer one.

Timothy, about this time, had been sent ahead by Paul into Macedonia with instructions to go on to Corinth (Acts 19:21-22; I Cor. 4:17). Paul urges the Corinthian church to welcome Timothy and to make his work as easy as possible while he is there (vv. 10-11).

Next, Paul explains the situation regarding Apollos. Evidently he is with Paul in Ephesus. Perhaps their letter had requested him to come.[1] Paul explains that he had urged Apollos to come but Apollos was unwilling. "Concerning the way in which Apollos had been made a rival to Paul in Corinth, it shows magnanimity on Paul's side to desire his return and a modest delicacy on the side of Apollos to decline the request."[2]

III. FINAL EXHORTATIONS AND GREETINGS (vv. 13-24)

As his custom was, Paul draws his letter to a close by a few general admonitions to steadfastness, courage, and strength. And in keeping with one of the major thrusts of this epistle he presses home their major need, "Let all that you do be done in love" (v. 14, NASB).

Among those who were present with Paul when he was writing this letter were three men from the Corinthian church. Probably they were the ones who had brought the Corinthian letter to him. It may be that they will be the bearers of this letter in reply. Paul acknowledges with gratitude the help and encouragement they have been to him, especially one of them, Stephanas, who with his family had been such a great help to Paul in the early days of the gospel at Corinth.

Next, greetings are passed on to the church at Corinth from (1) the churches of Asia, the many churches in the province where Paul has been working for the past three years; (2) from Aquila and Priscilla and the assembly of believers that met in their home, these were formerly of Corinth and would be well known there; (3) from all the brethren, the individual Christians who were able to send greetings. In response to these greetings

---

[1]This is based on the use of the formula "as touching our brother Apollos," the same formula in the original as found in 7:1; 8:1 and 16:1 for references to their letter.

[2]Findlay, *Expositor's Greek Testament*, p. 949.

the Corinthians were admonished to observe the customary holy kiss.

Last of all, Paul himself takes the pen from his secretary and writes with his own hand his own greetings. As he does so his heart is so filled with apprehension for the spiritual well-being of this church with all its problems that he bursts forth with one more admonition, "If any man love not the Lord Jesus Christ let him be Anathema [accursed, cf. 12:1-3; Gal. 1:8-9] Maranatha [our Lord is coming]."[3] The benediction of the grace of our Lord Jesus Christ and the reiteration of Paul's love for them closes the epistle.[4]

Questions for Discussion

1. Is social improvement a proper part of the gospel?

2. When, and by what means will all social problems be rectified?

3. Is tithing a valid principle for New Testament believers?

4. When did Christians start using the first day of the week instead of the seventh as their special day of meeting and worship? By whose authority?

5. Should the church insist on good businesslike methods of handling finances? Why?

6. Why do you suppose Paul bothered to include friendly greetings in his inspired writings? Does this say something important to us?

---

[3]Maranatha should not be taken together with Anathema. It is a sentence within itself, composed of two Aramaic words, the one meaning "our Lord" and the other a form of the verb "come." It is not certain whether it should be taken as a past tense, "our Lord has come," or a wish, "Oh, Lord, come," or present, "our Lord is coming." This last seems best in light of Philippians 4:5; James 5:7-8 and Revelation 1:7.

[4]The postscript added at the end of this and other of Paul's epistles in the KJV is not a part of the text, and is not found in our oldest manuscripts. It was an explanatory statement expressing the tradition of the later church regarding the circumstances of the writing of the epistle. "From Philippi" is almost certainly an error; Paul was in Ephesus. "By Stephanas, etc." means that they were the carriers who delivered the letter. This might well be true. But Timothy's name should be left out of that group, for he was not present.

SELECTED BIBLIOGRAPHY

Alford, Henry. *The Greek Testament*, II. London: Rivington, 1857.

Barclay, William. *The Letters to the Corinthians. The Daily Study Bible*. Philadelphia: The Westminster Press, 1954.

Barnes, Albert. *Barnes' Notes on the New Testament*. Edited by Ingram Cobbin. Grand Rapids: Kregel Publications, 1966.

Edwards, Thomas Charles. *A Commentary on the First Epistle to the Corinthians*. London: Hodder and Stoughton, 1897.

Erdman, Charles R. *The First Epistle of Paul to the Corinthians*. Philadelphia: The Westminster Press, 1928.

Findlay, G. G. "St. Paul's First Epistle to the Corinthians," *The Expositor's Greek Testament*, II. Edited by W. Robertson Nicoll. Grand Rapids: Wm. B. Eerdmans Publishing Co., 1939.

Godet, Frederick L. *Commentary on the First Epistle of St. Paul to the Corinthians*. Trans. by A. Cusin. Grand Rapids: Zondervan Publishing House, 1957.

Grosheide, F. W. *Commentary on the First Epistle to the Corinthians. New International Commentary on the New Testament*. Edited by N. B. Stonehouse. Grand Rapids: Wm. B. Eerdmans Publishing Co., 1953.

Hillyer, Norman. "1 and 2 Corinthians," *The New Bible Commentary: Revised*. Edited by D. Guthrie, et al. Grand Rapids: Wm. B. Eerdmans Publishing Co., 1970.

Hobbs, Herschel H. *The Epistles to the Corinthians*. Grand Rapids: Baker Book House, 1960.

Hodge, Charles. *An Exposition of the First Epistle to the Corinthians*. Grand Rapids: Wm. B. Eerdmans Publishing Co., 1950.

Johnson, S. Lewis. "The First Epistle to the Corinthians," *The Wycliffe Bible Commentary*. Edited by Charles F. Pfeiffer and Everett F. Harrison. Chicago: Moody Press, 1962.

Lenski, R. C. H. *The Interpretation of St. Paul's First and Second Epistle to the Corinthians*. Columbus, Ohio: Wartburg Press, 1946.

Marsh, Paul W. "I Corinthians," *A New Testament Commentary*. Edited by G. C. D. Howley. Grand Rapids: Zondervan Publishing House, 1969.

McFadyen, John Edgar. *The Epistles to the Corinthians*. London: Hodder and Stoughton, 1911.

McPheeters, Julian C. *The Epistles to the Corinthians. Proclaiming the New Testament.* Edited by Ralph G. Turnbull. Grand Rapids: Baker Book House, 1964.

Metz, Donald S. "I Corinthians," *Beacon Bible Commentary*, VIII. Edited by A. F. Harper, et. al. Kansas City: Beacon Hill Press, 1968.

Morgan, G. Campbell. *The Corinthian Letters of Paul.* New York: Revell Co., 1946.

Morris, Leon. *The First Epistle of Paul to the Corinthians. The Tyndale New Testament Commentaries.* Edited by R. V. G. Tasker. Grand Rapids: Wm. B. Eerdmans Publishing Co., 1958.

Robertson, Archibald Thomas. *Word Pictures in the New Testament*, IV. Nashville, Tenn.: Broadman Press, 1930.

Robertson, Archibald Thomas, and Plummer, Alfred. *A Critical and Exegetical Commentary on the First Epistle of St. Paul to the Corinthians. The International Critical Commentary.* Edited by Charles Augustus Briggs, Samuel Rolks Driver and Alfred Plummer. New York: Scribner's Sons, 1916.

Stanley, Arthur Penrhyn. *The Epistles of St. Paul to the Corinthians.* London: John Murray, 1876.

Vine, W. E. *I Corinthians.* London: Oliphants Ltd., 1951.